Faith Words
for KIDS
a DICTIONARY
for Parents, Teachers,
and Children

MELISSA K. HAMMER

BEACON HILL PRESS
OF KANSAS CITY

Copyright 2011
by Beacon Hill Press of Kansas City

ISBN 978-0-8341-2562-9

Printed in the
United States of America

Cover Design: Darlene Filley
Inside Design: Darlene Filley/Sharon Page

A Dictionary of the Bible & Christian Doctrine in Everyday English was used as background information for the terms and definitions of this book. Eby, J. Wesley; Lyons, George; Truesdale, Al; *A Dictionary of the Bible & Christian Doctrine in Everyday English,* copyright © 1986 and 2004, 2nd Edition (Beacon Hill Press of Kansas City).

10 9 8 7 6 5 4 3 2 1

DEDICATION

This book is dedicated to *Donna L. Fillmore*, retired Senior Editor, Children's Curriculum, Nazarene Publishing House. For more than thirty-seven years Donna tirelessly shared the faith and used words of the faith with children. She lived out Deuteronomy 6:7: "Impress them [commandments] on your children. Talk about them when you sit at home and when you walk along the road, when you lie down and when you get up."

And to my mother, Patricia Lynn Cochran Hammer, who early in my life instilled in me a love of words. Thanks for reading encyclopedias and dictionaries with me.

CONTENTS

ACKNOWLEDGMENTS

The author gratefully acknowledges the work of the Children's Curriculum editorial team (Nazarene Publishing House) and the team members of Children's Ministries International (Church of the Nazarene). The years that have been dedicated to defining words of the faith for children provided the detailed and age-appropriate definitions for this book.

The Pronunciation Guide used for the pronunciations of each word is courtesy of *A Dictionary of the Bible & Christian Doctrine in Everyday English.* Pronunciations of common words, such as care, are taken from *Merriam Webster's Collegiate Dictionary, 11th Edition.*

"Hear, O Israel: The LORD our God, the LORD is one.
Love the LORD your God with all your heart
and with all your soul and with all your strength.
These commandments that I give you today are to
be upon your hearts. Impress them on your children.
Talk about them when you sit at home
and when you walk along the road,
when you lie down and when you get up,"
(Deuteronomy 6:4-7).

INTRODUCTION

Do you remember the words that puzzled you as a child interacting within the church? Words such as *holy* (is that something full of holes?) or adoption (like the family who adopted Anya from Russia?). Do you remember listening to a salvation message and wondering, *What does it mean to be saved?* One word that always puzzled me was *faith.* People would say, "Just have faith." So what did that mean? Have faith? Is faith a tangible something to hold onto? How could I have something that I did not understand? A simple and direct definition would have been of tremendous help to me. "Just have faith" takes on new meaning when defined as "believing God's Word and acting in a way that shows that belief. Faith is trust in action." Ah, I am to have faith in God, whom I can trust, because His Word shows God to be trustworthy and promise-keeping. It all begins to fit together. . .

Kids are constantly hearing these words of the faith. The words that shape our understanding of who God is and how we are to live in right relationship with Him and with one another. Faith words and their well-defined and understood meanings are essential to spiritual formation.

Sometimes as these new words come at them, kids sit and wonder what the words could possibly mean. At other times, kids may come up with their own definitions as they listen to the context in which the words are spoken. These definitions can be right on, off-target, or a little sketchy. When you were a child did you ever have some odd explanations for words within the church that you did not quite understand? Or has your child ever asked that tough question from the back seat on your way home from a service, "What is atonement?" It can seem like children are playing a game of Stump the Grown-up at moments like this. Did you wish you had a handy reference guide to use?

This book is designed to be that handy reference guide. It can help you in two ways. One is to know which Faith Words are appropriate for introduction at what age level. The other is to provide you with age-appropriate definitions to use as a starting point for the tough conversations of the faith and for the everyday, ordinary conversations to help you define these words in context so that the next time your child asks, "What is atonement?" You can flip to the A words and start a conversation with the words, "Atonement, now that is a very good question to ask. Atonement can be described as all of God's actions, especially Jesus' suffering and death on the Cross, which makes it possible for people to be freed from sin and live in fellowship with God." Then you can move on to define sin and fellowship, and celebrate with your child that our Savior, Jesus Christ, has provided atonement for our sin. We can live and walk with God because of this. We can know of His love. What an excellent opportunity has opened for you to share salvation and the Christian life with your child.

It is my prayer that you will use this book in a variety of ways, but especially as a tool for conversational sparkers with kids. This is the fulfillment of the command found in Deuteronomy 6:6-7, "These commandments that I give you today are to be upon your hearts. Impress them on your children. Talk about them when you sit at home and when you walk along the road, when you lie down and when you get up."

May God bless as you continue the faith conversation,

Melissa

Melissa K. Hammer

HOW TO USE THIS BOOK

Age-Specific Lists

You will find on pages 16-23 graded lists of the specific words and their pronunciations. These lists are to provide for you, the parent or teacher, a quick reference as to what Faith Words are appropriate to address at what age. As with any age-graded list, it is important to remember that your child is unique. Your early-elementary-level child may ask about a word graded for preteens. This is okay. You may simply address the word, using or slightly modifying the definition given.

Alphabetical Dictionary of Words and Definitions

The alphabetical dictionary of the words chosen for use in this book begins on page 24. If your child asks about a specific word—for example the word sin—you may look up the word and its definitions. Use the age level that is appropriate for your child's age, education, and level of understanding. The pronunciation guide is given for each word to help you and your child learn the correct pronunciation for words of the faith. You will find a key for this guide beginning on page 14.

The age levels are identified within this section by the following code:

EC: Early Childhood definition	**ME:** Middle Elementary definition
EE: Early Elementary definition	**PT:** Preteen/Middle School definition

Primary Purpose for the Dictionary

The primary purpose for this dictionary is to provide you, parent or teacher, with an easy reference of church words, sometimes called "Christianese" to use in conversations with your children. Children hear words such as pastor, synagogue, sin, Golden Rule, and atonement as they interact with the community of faith. They may wonder what these words mean. They may come to you and ask. How will you respond? Hopefully you will transform your children's understanding of the faith by taking the time to say, "That is a good question to ask. Thank you for asking me. Let's find out together." Then pull out this book, find the word, read the appropriate definition, and ask, "What do you think about this?" Share the Scripture verse that is connected with the word. Read the verse together from this book or from the Bible. Continue the conversation with your child by sharing what this word means to you. Pray with your child, asking for God's continuing insight into His church and His Word.

ADDITIONAL IDEAS FOR USE

Flash Cards

Have you ever used word cards to teach your child important words? Perhaps you wrote the word stove on an index card and attached it to the stove. Every time you saw the word, you read it with your child. You can use this same concept with Faith Words. If you and your child have discussed a certain Faith Word, copy the card from the back of this book and add the definition. Place this card on the dash of your car. When you travel along the road, refer back to the word and continue the conversation as a family. God will grant new ideas and insight as together you work on the word. You will only want to continue this conversation for a few weeks. You do not want to overwhelm your child with two much information! The idea of teaching Faith Words is formational (to transform children) as well as informational (to transmit knowledge).

Faith Words Illustrations

Some of the words within this book will be good for illustration. Give your child a sheet of paper and then have your child draw an illustration of the Faith Word that you are talking about. Place this illustration in a place of importance in your home. Have your child explain the illustration to you using the Faith Word in a sentence.

Faith Words in Scripture

Some of the Faith Words appear in Scripture. When you are reading the Bible together, or participating in family devotional reading and a Faith Word appears, pause to review the definition together, and talk about what it means within the context of the Word of God.

You will also want to use the opportunity to talk about what this Faith Word means within the context of today. A verse is provided with each Faith Word. You can also look up verses in a concordance and share additional moments in the Word of God together as a family.

Remember: building an informed and comprehensive vocabulary is an important part of a child's development. This is also true for the words of the faith. The Church has a specialized vocabulary. Many of these words are used in other contexts, but in the Church they have special meanings that relate to the Christian faith.

It is important for children to learn the vocabulary of the Church along with Bible stories and Bible verses. They need this vocabulary to understand the Bible and Christian teaching. A child who does not know what sin is will not understand the verse "All have sinned and fall short of the glory of God" (Romans 3:23). In addition, the child will not really grasp the wonder of salvation if he or she does not understand sin and its seriousness.

As a parent and teacher, you have the God-given and ordained responsibility to teach the words of the faith so that children are transformed and live for Him. The Faith Words of this dictionary are a starting point. You can also refer to a Bible dictionary for help with words and terms that are not provided within this book.

Thank you for living out daily God's call of Deuteronomy 6 to "Impress them on your children. Talk about them when you sit at home and when you walk along the road, when you lie down and when you get up."

SIMPLE "FAMILY TIME" DEVOTIONS PLAN

"Think About It" Family Time

You will find more than cut and dried definitions in this dictionary! Along with the age level definitions supplied, each word has a scripture with it, along with a "Think About It" conversation starter.

You can simply use this book for weekly family devotions:

1. Choose a weekly word to learn, review, and talk about as a family. This will mean 52 words of the faith learned in a one year time frame.
2. Each week have a family member introduce the chosen word, read it, and read the definition.
3. Look up the Bible verse printed with the word. Have a family member read it aloud.
4. Introduce the "Think About It" conversation starter. Talk about the word, definition, verse, and conversation starter together. Encourage each family member to give input.
5. At the close of the week, ask each family member to share how the Faith Word for the week has had an influence on choices, thoughts, or attitudes.

PRONUNCIATION GUIDE

VOWELS

SYMBOL	KEY WORDS	USUAL SPELLINGS
ay	age, day	a, ai, ay
a	ask, back	a
ah	father, ox	a, o
aw	auto, saw	au, aw
ee	each, sea	e, ee, ea, ey, y
e	egg, bed	e
air	air, bear	air, are, ear
er	her, bird, fur	er, ir, ur
ie	ice, pie, my	i, ie, y
i	inch, sit	i
oh	oat, nose	o, oa, oe, ow
ew	new, moon	u, ew, oo, ue
oo	good, bush	oo, u
ou	out, cow	ou, ow
oy	oil, boy	oi, oy
yew	use, human	u
u or uh*	up, just, sofa	u, a, e, i, o

CONSONANTS

SYMBOL	KEY WORDS	USUAL SPELLINGS
b	boat, cab	b, bb
ch	church, match	ch, tch
d	day, dad	d, dd
f	foot, wife	f, ff, ph, gh
g	gate, big	g, gg
h	hand, behind	h, wh
j	joy, page	j, g, dg
k	king, music	k, c, ck, ch
ks	box, sacks	x, cks
kw	queen, equal	qu
l	life, hill	l, ll
m	man, ham	m, mm
n	new, son	n, nn, kn
ng	drink, sing	n, ng
p	pig, cap	p, pp
r	race, year	r, rr, wr
s	sun, face	s, c, ss, sc
sh	sheep, fish	sh, ch, ti
t	teach, mat	t, tt
th	thin, bath	th
th	this, bathe	th
v	vine, give	v
w	win, away	w
y	you, lawyer	y
z	zeal, breeze	z
zh	treasure, azure	s, z

*Same as the schwa sound found in many dictionaries.

PRESCHOOL AND KINDERGARTEN, PRE-READERS

This list of 28 words is recommended for faith conversation sparkers with young children, pre-readers, ages 3-6. Of course, as children of any age ask questions about words they have heard, you can give them a basic answer that will satisfy curiosity and lay in place the foundation for greater understanding as the child matures.

Advent (AD-vent)
Altar (AWL-ter)
Bible (BIE-bul)
Christmas (KRIS-mus)
Church (CHERCH)
Creator (kree-AY-ter)
Easter (EE-ster)
Follower of Jesus (FAH-luh-wer of JEE-zus)
Friend (FREND)
God (GAHD)
God's care (GAHD's KAIR)
God's help (GAHD's HELP)
God's power (GAHD's POW-er)
Good Friday (GOOD FRI-day)
Good news (GOOD NEWZ)

Jesus (JEE-zus)
Love (LUV)
Miracle (MIR-uh-kul)
Obey (oh-BAY)
Offering (AWF-er-ing)
Palm Sunday (PAHM SUN-dee)
Parable(s) (PAIR-uh-bul)
Power (POW-ur)
Praise (PRAYZ)
Prayer (PRAYR)
Promise (PRAHM-is)
Trust (TRUST)
Worship (WER-shup)

FIRST AND SECOND GRADERS, LEVEL 1 READERS, AGES 6-8

EE

This list of 54 words is recommended for faith conversation sparkers with early elementary children, beginning readers, ages 6-8. Of course, as children of any age ask questions about words they have heard, you can give them a basic answer that will satisfy curiosity and lay in place the foundation for greater understanding as the child matures. Faith Words are meant to be an ongoing conversation between you and your child.

Advent (AD-vent)
Altar (AWL-ter)
Anoint (uh-NOYNT)
Ascension (uh-SEN-shun)
Believers (buh-LEE-vers)
Bible (BIE-bul)
Christ (KRIEST)
Church (CHERCH)
Community (kuh-MYEW-nuh-tee)
Covet (KUV-it)
Creator (kree-AY-ter)
Crucifixion (KREW-suh-FIK-shun)
Disciple(s) (duh-SIE-pulz)
Eternal life (ee-TER-nul LIEF)
Exodus (EK-suh-dus)
Faith (FAYTH)
Faithful (FAYTH-ful)
Follower of Jesus (FAH-luh-wer of JEE-zus)
God (GAHD)

God's power (GAHD's POW-er)
God's work (GAHD's WERK)
Heaven (HEV-un)
Honor (ON-er)
Jesus (JEE-zus)
Kingdom of God (KING-dum of GAHD)
Love (LUV)
Miracle (MIR-uh-kul)
Obey (oh-BAY)
Offering (AWF-er-ing)
Parable (PAIR-uh-bul)
Passover (PAS-OH-ver)
Pastor (PAS-ter)
Peace with God (PEES with GAHD)
Pentecost (PEN-tuh-kawst)
Pray (PRAY)
Prayer (PRAYR)
Promise (PRAHM-is)
Prophet (PRAH-fut)

Resurrection (REZ-uh-REK-shun)
Righteous (RIE-chus)
Sabbath (SAB-uth)
Sacrifice (SAK-ruh-FIES)
Salvation (sal-VAY-shun)
Sanctuary (SANG-chew-AIR-ee)
Saved (SAYVD)
Savior (SAYV-yer)
Sin (SIN)

Son of God (SUN of GAHD)
Temptation (temp-TAY-shun)
Ten Commandments
    (TEN kuh-MAND-munts)
Testify (TES-tuh-FIE)
Trust (TRUST)
Wisdom (WIZ-dum)
Worship (WER-shup)

THIRD AND FOURTH GRADERS, LEVEL 2/3 READERS, AGES 8-10

This list of 100 words is recommended for faith conversation sparkers with middle elementary children, middle to advanced readers, ages 8-11. Of course, as children of any age ask questions about words they have heard, you can give them a basic answer that will satisfy curiosity and lay in place the foundation for greater understanding as the child matures. Faith Words are meant to be an ongoing conversation between you and your child throughout the childhood and teen years. This is not an exhaustive list, but a starting point. Look to other Bible and Christian dictionaries for additional words.

Accountable (uh-COUNT-uh-bul)
Advent (AD-vent)
Altar (AWL-ter)
Apostle (uh-PAHS-ul)
Armor of God (AHR-mer of GAHD)
Ascension (uh-SEN-shun)
Bible (BIE-bul)
Blessing (BLES-ing)
Body of Christ (BAH-dee of KRIEST)
Choice(s) (CHOYS)
Christian (KRIS-chun)
Church (CHERCH)
Commandment (kuh-MAND-munt)
Commit/Commitment
   (kuh-MITT/kuh-MITT-munt)
Compassion (kum-PA-shum)
Consecrate (KAHN-see-krayt)
Conviction (kun-VIK-shun)
Covenant (KUV-uh-nunt)

Covet (KUV-it)
Create (kree-AYT)
Creator (kree-AY-ter)
Cross (KRAHS)
Disciple(s) (duh-SIE-pulz)
Eternal life (ee-TER-nul LIEF)
Evil (EE-vul)
Faith (FAYTH)
Faithful (FAYTH-ful)
Fast (FAST)
Fear (FEER)
Forgive (fohr-GIV)
Forgiveness (fohr-GIV-nus)
Gentile (JEN-tiel)
God (GAHD)
God's power (GAHD's POW-er)
God's will (GAHD's WIL)
Golden Rule (GOHL-dun REWL)
Gospel (GAHS-pul)

MIDDLE ELEMENTARY WORD LIST

ME

Grace (GRAYS)
Gracious (GRAY-shus)
Hallowed (HAL-oh-ed)
Heart (HAHRT)
Heaven (HEV-un)
Holy (HOH-lee)
Holy Spirit (HOH-lee SPIR-ut)
Honor (ON-er)
Hope (HOHP)
Idol (IE-dul)
Image of God (IM-ij of GAHD)
Immanuel (i-MAN-yuh-wul)
Inspiration (IN-spuh-RAY-shun)
Jealousy (JEL-uh-see)
Jesus (JEE-zus)
Judge (JUJ)
Kingdom of God (KING-dum of GAHD)
Lord's Prayer (LOHRDZ PRAYR)
Love (LUV)
Mercy (MER-see)
Messiah (muh-SIE-uh)
Miracle (MIR-uh-kul)
Missionary (MISH-uh-NAIR-ee)
Obey (oh-BAY)
Obedience (oh-BEE-dee-uns)
Offering (AWF-er-ing)
Outreach (OUT-REECH)
Pagan (PAY-gun)
Parable (PAIR-uh-bul)
Pardon (PAHR-dun)
Passover (PAS-OH-ver)
Patriarch (PAY-tree-ahrk)

Pentecost (PEN-tuh-kawst)
Persecution (PER-suh-KYEW-shun)
Pharisees (FAIR-uh-SEEZ)
Praise (PRAYZ)
Prayer (PRAYR)
Promise (PRAHM-is)
Prophecy (PRAHF-uh-see)
Prophet (PRAH-fut)
Redeem (ree-DEEM)
Refuge (reh-FEWJ)
Repent (ree-PENT)
Repentance (ree-PEN-tuns)
Restitution (RES-tuh-TEW-shun)
Resurrection (REZ-uh-REK-shun)
Revere (reh-VEER)
Righteous (RIE-chus)
Sabbath (SAB-uth)
Sacred (SAY-krud)
Sacrifice (SAK-ruh-fies)
Salvation (sal-VAY-shun)
Savior (SAYV-yer)
Second coming (SEK-und KUM-ing)
Sin (SIN)
Son of Man (SUN of MAN)
Sovereign (SAHV-run)
Submission (sub-MI-shun)
Temptation (temp-TAY-shun)
Trust (TRUST)
Wisdom (WIZ-dum)
Witness (WIT-nus)
Worship (WER-shup)

FIFTH—SEVENTH GRADERS, LEVEL 3 PROFICIENT/ADVANCED READERS, AGES 11-13

This list of 146 words is recommended for faith conversation sparkers with preteen and middle school students, advanced readers, ages 11-13. This age group is in the process of becoming analytical thinkers. They are questioning areas of faith. The Faith Words offered here are meant to be an ongoing conversation between you and your young teen. It is a conversation that will continue throughout life. This is not an exhaustive list, but a starting point. Look to other Bible and Christian dictionaries for additional words. Encourage your young teen to do the same.

PT

Abomination (uh-BAHM-uh-NAY-shun)
Acceptance (ik-SEP-tuns)
Accountable (uh-KOUN-tuh-bul)
Adoption (uh-DAHP-shun)
Advent (AD-vent)
Advocate (AD-vuh-kut)
Agape (ah-GAH-pay)
Altar (AWL-ter)
Anoint (uh-NOYNT)
Antichrist (AN-ti-KRIEST)
Apostle (uh-PAHS-ul)
Ascension (uh-SEN-shun)
Assurance (uh-SHOOR-uns)
Atonement (uh-TOHN-munt)
Atoning sacrifice
        (uh-TOHN-ing SAK-ruh-fies)
Baptism (BAP-tiz-um)
Blessed (BLESD)

Blessing (BLES-ing)
Body of Christ (BAH-dee of KRIEST)
Born Again (BOHRN uh-GEN)
Canon (KAN-un)
Christ/Messiah (KRIEST/muh-SIE-uh)
Christian (KRIS-chun)
Church (CHERCH)
Comforter (KUM-fer-ter)
Commandment (kuh-MAND-munt)
Commit (kuh-MIT)
Commitment (kuh-MIT-munt)
Communion (kuh-MYEWN-yun)
Compassion (kum-PA-shun)
Condemn (kun-DEM)
Confess (kun-FES)
Consecrate (KAHN-see-KRAYT)
Convict (kun-VIKT)
Covenant (KUV-uh-nunt)

PT

Covet (KUV-it)
Create (kree-AYT)
Creator (kree-AY-ter)
Creed (KREED)
Deity (DEE-uh-tee)
Disciple (duh-SIE-pul)
Divine (duh-VIEN)
Entire Sanctification
    (EN-tier SANG-tuh-fuh-KAY-shun)
Eternal life (ee-TER-nul LIEF)
Eternity (ee-TER-nuh-tee)
Eucharist (YEW-kuh-rust)
Evangelism (ee-VAN-juh-liz-um)
Evangelist (ee-VAN-juh-list)
Evil (EE-vuhl)
Faith (FAYTH)
Faithful (FAYTH-ful)
Fall (FAWL)
Family of God (FAM-uh-lee of GAHD)
Fellowship (FEL-oh-ship)
Fool (FEWL)
Forgive (fohr-GIV)
Forgiveness (fohr-GIV-nus)
Free will (FREE WIL)
Fruit of the Spirit (FREWT of the SPIR-it)
Glorify (GLOH-ruh-fie)
Godliness (GAHD-lee-nus)
Gospel (GAHS-pul)
Grace (GRAYS)
Growth in grace (GROHTH in GRAYS)
High Priest (HIE PREEST)

Holiness (HOH-lee-nus)
Holy (HOH-lee)
Holy Spirit (HOH-lee SPIR-it)
Honor (ON-er)
Hope (HOHP)
Hypocrisy (hi-PAHK-ruh-see)
Image of God (IM-ij of GAHD)
Immanuel (i-MAN-yuh-wul)
Incarnation (IN-kahr-NAY-shun)
Intercede (IN-ter-SEED)
Jesus (JEE-zus)
Joy (JOY)
Judge (JUJ)
Judgment (JUJ-munt)
Justification (JUS-tuh-fuh-KAY-shun)
Kingdom of God (KING-dum of GAHD)
Law (LAW)
Lord's Supper (LOHRDZ SUP-er)
Love (LUV)
Mediator (MEE-dee-AY-ter)
Meek (MEEK)
Mercy (MER-see)
Miracle (MIR-uh-kul)
Missionary (MISH-un-NAIR-ee)
Missions (MISH-uns)
Mourn (MORN)
Obey (oh-BAY)
Original sin (uh-RIJ-uh-nul SIN)
Parable (PAIR-uh-bul)
Passover (PAS-OH-ver)
Patriarch (PAY-tree-ahrk)

Peacemaker (PEES-MAYK-er)
Pentecost (PEN-tuh-kawst)
Perish (PAIR-ish)
Persecution (PER-suh-KYEW-shun)
Perseverance (PER-suh-VIR-uns)
Poor in spirit (POR in SPIR-it)
Prayer (PRAYR)
Prevenient grace (pree-VEEN-yunt GRAYS)
Priest (PREEST)
Promise (PRAHM-is)
Prophecy (PRAHF-uh-see)
Pure in heart (PYOOR in HAHRT)
Redeem (ree-DEEM)
Redeemer (ree-DEEM-er)
Regeneration (REE-jen-er-AY-shun)
Repent (ree-PENT)
Repentance (ree-PEN-tuns)
Restitution (RES-tuh-TEW-shun)
Resurrection (REZ-uh-REK-shun)
Reverence (REV-er-uns)
Righteous (RIE-chus)
Righteousness (RIE-chus-nes)
Sabbath (SAB-uth)
Sacrament (SAK-ruh-munt)
Sacrifice (SAK-ruh-fies)
Salvation (sal-VAY-shun)

Sanctification (SANG-tuh-fuh-KAY-shun)
Sanctify (SANG-tuh-fie)
Savior (SAYV-yer)
Second coming (SEK-und KUM-ing)
Sin (SIN)
Sovereign (SAHV-run)
Spiritual gifts (SPIR-uh-chuh-wul GIFTS)
Stewardship (STEW-erd-ship)
Synagogue (SIN-uh-gahg)
Temple (TEM-pul)
Tempt (TEMPT)
Temptation (temp-TAY-shun)
Tithe (TIE<u>TH</u>)
Transgress (tranz-GRES)
Trinity (TRIN-uh-tee)
Trust (TRUST)
Unconditional love (un-cun-DI-shu-nul LUV)
Unity (YEW-nuh-tee)
Unrighteous (un-RIE-chus)
Witness (WIT-nus)
Witness of the Spirit (WIT-nus of the SPIR-it)
Worldly passion (WERLD-lee PA-shun)
Worship (WER-shup)

Please remember that not every word will be appropriate to introduce at every age level. However, once a word is introduced it can be communicated and expanded upon throughout each age level. One way to continue the conversation with your child is to ask about specific words, what those words mean, and how the words are used as a part of the Church and a part of your child's life.

EC: Early Childhood definition

EE: Early Elementary definition

ME: Middle Elementary definition

PT: Preteen/Middle School definition

Abomination
(uh-BAHM-uh-NAY-shun)

PT: An **abomination** is something or someplace that is sinful. It is an offense to God. When people put other things in place of God this is an **abomination**. For example, worshiping false gods or setting up idols is an **abomination**.

"The images of their gods you are to burn in the fire. Do not covet the silver and gold on them, and do not take it for yourselves, or you will be ensnared by it, for it is detestable to the LORD your God," (Deuteronomy 7:25).

Think About It: God should always be first in your life, in your worship, and in importance. Anything else is detestable or an **abomination**.

Acceptance (ik-SEP-tuns)

Note: Before the preteen age this is demonstrated to children through actions and words. They experience and learn to offer **acceptance** through parents and other teachers.

PT: Welcoming and showing love to others as they are. As Christians, we are to **accept** everyone, even when we cannot agree with them or approve of what they do.

*"**Accept** one another, then, just as Christ **accepted** you, in order to bring praise to God,"* (Romans 15:7).

Think About It: You have Jesus' love and **acceptance**. He makes you whole. You can give this love and wholeness to others as you show them Jesus' love.

Accountable
(uh-KOUN-tuh-bul)

Note: Before middle elementary age, children learn responsibility through the teaching guidance of parents and other teachers.

ME/PT: To be responsible for one's actions.

*"Nothing in all creation is hidden from God's sight. Everything is uncovered and laid bare before the eyes of him to whom we must give **account**," (Hebrews 4:13).*

Think About It: Taking responsibility for what you do and say and think is a part of growing up. You also grow as a Christian when you admit your responsibility to obey God.

Adoption (uh-DAHP-shun)

PT: God's action to make the repentant sinner His very own child.

"I will be a Father to you, and you will be my sons and daughters, says the Lord Almighty," (2 Corinthians 6:18).

Think About It: You know that your mom and dad love you. God loves you even more! You are God's child when you choose to love, serve, and obey Him. He becomes your Father.

Advent (AD-vent)

EC: The four weeks before Christmas.

EE: The four weeks before Christmas when Christians prepare to celebrate Jesus' birth.

ME: A word that means "coming." The four weeks before Christmas are the **Advent** season when Christians prepare to celebrate the birth of Christ.

PT: A word that means "coming." The four weeks before Christmas are the **Advent** season when Christians prepare to celebrate the birth of Christ. This preparation may include praying, fasting, and thinking about one's spiritual life.

"An angel of the Lord appeared to them, and the glory of the Lord shone around them, and they were terrified. But the angel said to them, 'Do not be afraid. I bring you good news of great joy that will be for all the people. Today in the town of David a Savior has been born to you; he is Christ the Lord,'" (Luke 2:9-11).

Think About It: Advent is a special time when we anticipate or look forward to the celebration of the good news that Jesus, our Savior, is come! How do you and your family celebrate this special time?

Advocate (AD-vuh-kut)

PT: One who speaks on the behalf of another. The Holy Spirit speaks for God to the world. Jesus speaks on our behalf to God, the Father.

"My dear children, I write this to you so that you will not sin. But if anybody does sin, we have one who speaks to the Father in our defense—Jesus Christ, the Righteous One," (1 John 2:1).

Think About It: Who is someone that helps you when you need help? This person speaks to others for you. Like when Mom or Dad talks to the doctor and tells her what is wrong when you are sick. The Holy Spirit is an **advocate**. He speaks to you. He helps you know what God wants for you. Jesus is an **advocate** too. He talks to God, the Father, for you. When you pray, you can know that God hears.

Agape (ah-GAH-pay)

PT: This word means love. It is Greek. It is used in the New Testament to describe God's love and Christian love that loves without expectation of love in return.

"'Love the Lord your God with all your heart and with all your soul and with all your strength and with all your mind'; and, 'Love your neighbor as yourself,'" (Luke 10:27).

Think About It: Who do you know that loves you? Do you return that love? Do you know that God loves you. He is the ultimate love. God loves all people, even those who do not love Him in return.

Altar (AWL-ter)

Note: This word can be confusing for children. They learn of altars in the Old Testament, and then they see altars within the church today.

EC: The **altar** is a place set aside where people can worship and talk with God.

EE: The **altar** can be used to sacrifice to God, as in the Old Testament. It is a place where people talk with God and ask forgiveness.

ME: The **altar** is a place where people sacrifice to gods. The **altar** of the Old Testament is where people sacrificed to and worshiped the one true God. Jesus became the once and for all time sacrifice. Christians live their lives to be pleasing to God. The **altar** in a church of today is where people seek forgiveness from God for sin, and talk with Him.

PT: The **altar** is a place where people sacrifice to gods. The **altar** of the Old Testament is where people sacrificed to and worshiped the one true God. Jesus became the once and for all time sacrifice. Christians live their lives as "living sacrifices" obediently living to be pleasing to God. The **altar** in a church of today is where people seek forgiveness from God for sin, and talk with Him.

"Follow my example, as I follow the example of Christ," (1 Corinthians 11:1).

Think About It: What are the different types of **altars** that you have seen or heard about? What do you think it means to live to please God so that each day you are putting your whole self on the **altar**?

Anoint (uh-NOYNT)

EL/ME: To put oil on someone's head. Kings, priests, and prophets were **anointed** in the Bible. This act showed that God had chosen them to do something special [important] for Him.

PT: To put oil on a person for healing purposes or to show that the person has been called to serve God in a special way. We also say that God **anoints** us when He gives us His Holy Spirit.

*"Is any one of you sick? He should call the elders of the church to pray over him and **anoint** him with oil in the name of the Lord," (James 5:14).*

Think About It: Have you ever been in a service when someone who needed to be healed was **anointed** with oil? This is one way we can show that we believe in God's faithfulness and power to heal. We can also trust in God to **anoint** us to live for Him. This happens when God calls us to do something special. Do you know anyone **anointed** to serve God?

Note: There are times that two age levels are presented together. This simply means that depending upon the development of your child, you can introduce a word successfully with the given definition at either age.

Antichrist (AN-ti-KRIEST)

PT: Any group, individual, or movement that denies Jesus Christ is God's Son and the Savior of the world.

*"Who is the liar? It is the man who denies that Jesus is the Christ. Such a man is the **antichrist**—he denies the Father and the Son. No one who denies the Son has the Father; whoever acknowledges the Son has the Father also," (1 John 2:22-23).*

Think About It: What are some ways that people deny Jesus as the Son of God? How do you show your belief in Jesus as the Son of God?

Note: The antichrist named in the book of Revelation is the enemy of Jesus. This is something that can be confusing for children and is generally not recommended for discussion in childhood.

Apostle (uh-PAHS-ul)

ME/PT: One who is "sent out" on a special mission for another person. Jesus called certain people to be His **apostles**. These included the 12 disciples and Paul. The task of the **apostles** was to preach the gospel so people would become followers of Jesus Christ.

*"It was he who gave some to be **apostles**, some to be prophets, some to be evangelists, and some to be pastors and teachers, to prepare God's people for works of service, so that the body of Christ may be built up," (Ephesians 4:11-12).*

Think About It: God called the first **apostles**. God still calls you to live for Him and share Jesus' love with others. What is one way that you show Jesus' love?

Armor of God
(AHR-mer of GAHD)

ME: Our protection against evil. When we put on this **armor** we can stand strong against temptation, and make right choices each day.

*"Finally, be strong in the Lord and in his mighty power. Put on the full **armor of God** so that you can take your stand against the devil's schemes. For our struggle is not against flesh and blood, but against the rulers, against the authorities, against the powers of this dark world and against the spiritual forces of evil in the heavenly realms. Therefore put on the full **armor of God**, so that when the day of evil comes, you may be able to stand your ground, and after you have done everything, to stand,"* (Ephesians 6:10-13).

Think About It: Read Ephesians 6:10-18 with your family. Talk about how the **armor of God** helps you to live with courage for Him.

Ascension (uh-SEN-shun)

EE: Jesus' **ascension** was when He returned to heaven to be with God.

ME/PT: Ascend means to move upward. The **ascension** of Jesus Christ was when He "moved upward" and returned to heaven after His resurrection.

"He [Jesus] was taken up before their very eyes, and a cloud hid him from their sight. They were looking intently up into the sky as he was going, when suddenly two men dressed in white stood beside them. 'Men of Galilee,' they said, 'why do you stand here looking into the sky? This same Jesus, who has been taken from you into heaven, will come back in the same way you have seen him go into heaven,'" (Acts 1:9-11).

Think About It: Have you ever imagined what it will be like when Jesus returns? How would you describe His return? How does it feel to know Jesus will return?

Assurance (uh-SHOOR-uns)

PT: The Holy Spirit gives **assurance** or certainty of salvation to people who believe in Jesus Christ and accept Him as Lord and Savior.

"Let us draw near to God with a sincere heart in full assurance of faith, having our hearts sprinkled to cleanse us from a guilty conscience and having our bodies washed with pure water. Let us hold unswervingly to the hope we profess, for he who promised is faithful," (Hebrews 10:22-23).

Think About It: God is unswervingly faithful. That means we can count on Him not to change. How do you count on God to keep His promises?

Atonement (uh-TOHN-munt)

PT: All of God's actions, especially Jesus' suffering and death on the Cross, which made it possible for people to be freed from sin and live in fellowship with God.

"For this reason he had to be made like his brothers in every way, in order that he might become a merciful and faithful high priest in service to God, and that he might make atonement for the sins of the people," (Hebrews 2:17).

Think About It: What can you say to Jesus for His work of **atonement**? How can you live to be more like Him?

Atoning sacrifice (uh-TOHN-ing SAK-ruh-fies)

PT: The ultimate **atoning sacrifice** was Jesus' suffering and death on the Cross, which makes it possible for repentant sinners to receive forgiveness of sin by faith.

"For even the Son of Man did not come to be served, but to serve, and to give his life as a ransom for many," (Mark 10:45).

Think About It: Jesus' death on the Cross makes it possible for your forgiveness. How can you praise Jesus for this **atoning sacrifice** in something that you do today?

Baptism (BAP-tiz-um)

PT: A sacrament in which a believer is immersed in water or has water sprinkled or poured on his or her head. It symbolizes and gives public testimony to God's forgiveness, the believer's repentance, receiving the Holy Spirit, and beginning a new life in Christ.

*"There is one body and one Spirit—just as you were called to one hope when you were called—one Lord, one faith, one **baptism**; one God and Father of all, who is over all and through all and in all. But to each one of us grace has been given as Christ apportioned it," (Ephesians 4:4-7).*

Think About It: Baptism is a sacrament. You can find sacrament in this dictionary. Have you been baptized? What did it mean for you? Would you like to consider **baptism**? Talk to your family and pastor.

Note: when your child expresses interest in Christian Baptism, it is appropriate to talk about the meaning of the word and the process that will occur. You may have also chosen infant baptism.

Believers (buh-LEE-vers)

EE: People who believe that Jesus is God's Son. **Believers** have received Jesus as their Savior, and they love and obey Him.

*"All the **believers** were one in heart and mind. No one claimed that any of his possessions was his own, but they shared everything they had," (Acts 4:32).*

Think About It: Who are the **believers** that you know? How do you know they believe in Jesus? How do you show that you are a **believer**?

Bible (RIE-bul)

EC: The Bible is a special book that teaches us about God and helps us know Him.

EE: God's special book. The **Bible** tells us about God and helps us know Him. It shows how He wants us to live.

ME: The inspired Word of God, containing the 66 books of the Old and New Testaments. God reveals himself through the **Bible** and shows us how to love and serve Him.

"Now the Bereans were of more noble character than the Thessalonians, for they received the message with great eagerness and examined the Scriptures every day to see if what Paul said was true," (Acts 17:11).

Think About It: You have responsibility. That's right. To obey and live according to what God teaches in the **Bible**, you have to read it and pray for His guidance in your choices. You can do it!

Blessed (BLESD)

PT: Enjoying God's approval and experiencing spiritual joy as a result.

*"**Blessed** are those who dwell in your house; they are ever praising you. **Blessed** are those whose strength is in you, who have set their hearts on pilgrimage," (Psalm 84:4-5).*

Think About It: We are **blessed** or experience great joy that is deeper than any feeling or circumstance when we love, obey, and serve God.

Blessing (BLES-ing)

ME/PT: A good gift from God that brings joy, such as mercy, approval, or another kind of gift.

*"I will **bless** them and the places surrounding my hill. I will send down showers in season; there will be showers of **blessing,**"* (Ezekiel 34:26).

Think About It: Living into God's will for your life is a **blessing**. How might you tell others about God's approval and **blessing**?

Body of Christ (BAH-dee of KRIEST)

ME/PT: All believers working together under Christ's direction, each with different gifts and abilities, to build the kingdom of God.

"Just as each of us has one body with many members, and these members do not all have the same function, so in Christ we who are many form one body, and each member belongs to all the others," (Romans 12:4-5).

Think About It: What is something you do well? How could you do this to share the love of Jesus with others? You are a part of the **body of Christ**. You get to share His love!

Born Again (BOHRN uh-GEN)

PT: A work of God in which a repentant sinner receives spiritual life, which is a personal relationship with God.

*"Jesus declared, 'I tell you the truth, no one can see the kingdom of God unless he is **born again**,'" (John 3:3).*

Think About it: Have you asked Jesus to be your Savior? Tell someone about it!

Canon (KAN-un)

PT: A list of the books of the Bible, the inspired written Word of God. There are 66 books in the Protestant Bible, Old Testament and New Testament.

"All Scripture is God-breathed and is useful for teaching, rebuking, correcting and training in righteousness, so that the man of God may be thoroughly equipped for every good work," (2 Timothy 3:16-17).

Think About It: The Bible is the inspired written Word of God. What do you think that means for how you are to interact with it?

Choice(s) (CHOYS)

ME: Decisions about what to do. We make right **choices** when we obey God. We make wrong **choices** when we disobey God.

*"If anyone **chooses** to do God's will, he will find out whether my teaching comes from God or whether I speak on my own. He who speaks on his own does so to gain honor for himself, but he who works for the honor of the one who sent him is a man of truth; there is nothing false about him,"* (John 7:17-18).

Think About It: How can your right **choices** bring honor to God? How do wrong **choices** dishonor God?

Christ (KRIEST)

EE: A special name for Jesus. **Christ** means "chosen by God." God chose Jesus **Christ** to be our Savior.

*"Simon Peter answered, 'You are the **Christ**, the Son of the living God,'"* (Matthew 16:16).

Think About It: Jesus is the **Christ**. He is God's Son and our Savior. Have you chosen to accept Jesus **Christ** as your Lord and Savior?

Christ/Messiah
(KRIEST/muh-SIE-uh)

PT: **Christ** is a Greek word and **Messiah** is a Hebrew word. Both mean "the Anointed One," and they both refer to Jesus.

*"The first thing Andrew did was to find his brother Simon and tell him, 'We have found the **Messiah**' (that is, the **Christ**). And he brought him to Jesus," (John 1:41-42).*

Think About It: When you hear Jesus called **Messiah**, what do you think that means? How does it feel to know that the **Messiah** knows and loves you?

Christian (KRIS-chun)

ME/PT: A person who has been born again. A **Christian** has repented of sin, received Jesus Christ as Savior and Lord, and obeys Him.

*"When he found him, he brought him to Antioch. So for a whole year Barnabas and Saul met with the church and taught great numbers of people. The disciples were called **Christians** first at Antioch," (Acts 11:26).*

Think About It: To be called a **Christian** means that you are identified as a follower of Jesus Christ. What a great honor! How do people know you are a **Christian**?

Christmas (KRIS-mus)

EC: **Christmas** is a special time when Christians celebrate the birthday of Jesus, God's Son.

"Today in the town of David a Savior has been born to you; he is Christ the Lord," (Luke 2:11).

Think About It: The angels celebrated the first **Christmas** with announcements and song. How do you celebrate Jesus' birth during the season of Advent and as a part of **Christmas**?

Church (CHERCH)

EC: The **Church** is the people who know and love God and His Son, Jesus. The place where we worship God is also called a **church**.

EE: God's family of believers who have received Jesus as Savior. The **Church** with a capital C is all believers, everywhere. The **church** can also mean a place of worship.

ME: The community of people who trust Jesus as Savior and seek to build His kingdom. When used with a small initial c, **church** also means a place of worship or a group that meets regularly for worship and fellowship. When used with a capital C, **Church** means all believers. The **Church** is also called the body of Christ.

PT: The community of people who trust Jesus as Savior and seek to build His kingdom. When used with a small initial c, **church** also means a place of worship, a group that meets regularly for worship and fellowship, or a denomination. When used with a capital C, **Church** means all believers. The **Church** is also called the Body of Christ.

*"He [Jesus] is before all things, and in him all things hold together. And he is the head of the body, the **church**; he is the beginning and the firstborn from among the dead, so that in everything he might have the supremacy," (Colossians 1:17-18).*

Think About It: Jesus is our head. He directs us. He holds us together when we become a part of the **Church**. We are His people. How does being a part of Jesus' **church** change how you live?

Comforter (KUM-fer-ter)

PT: This is another title given to the Holy Spirit. It means that the Holy Spirit is with Christians, giving them encouragement.

"And hope does not disappoint us, because God has poured out his love into our hearts by the Holy Spirit, whom he has given us," (Romans 5:5).

Think About It: Jesus promised we would not be alone. He gives us the gift of the Holy Spirit. This is God with us today. He is our **comforter**. How do you sense the **comfort** of the Holy Spirit in tough times?

Commandment
(kuh-MAND-munt)

ME: A law given by God that tells people how to live.

PT: A law or instruction given by God that tells people how to live—for example, the Ten **Commandments**.

*"Now all has been heard; here is the conclusion of the matter: Fear God and keep his **commandments**, for this is the whole duty of man," (Ecclesiastes 12:13).*

Think About It: God teaches us how to live and His expectation for us is to live daily in obedience to Him. How do you obey God each day?

Commit/Commitment
(kuh-MIT/kuh-MIT-munt)

ME/PT: A promise or agreement to do something; to give yourself fully to a person or a cause.

*"**Commit** your way to the LORD; trust in him and he will do this:*

He will make your righteousness shine like the dawn, the justice of your cause like the noonday sun," (Psalm 37:5).

Think About It: God makes a **commitment** or promise to be with us. When we **commit** to God, we are promising that we will live for Him. How has being **committed** or promised to God changed your life?

Communion
(kuh-MYEWN-yun)

PT: A sacrament in which Christians eat bread and drink wine or grape juice. The bread symbolizes Jesus' body and the wine symbolizes His blood. When we take part in **communion** we remember Christ's death and look forward to His second coming. We celebrate Christ's special presence with us when we take **communion.**

"And he took bread, gave thanks and broke it, and gave it to them, saying, 'This is my body given for you; do this in remembrance of me.' In the same way, after the supper he took the cup, saying, 'This cup is the new covenant in my blood, which is poured out for you,'" (Luke 22:19-20).

Think About It: When we participate in **communion**, we are remembering what Jesus did for us and taking part in the new covenant or the promise that Jesus is our Savior and Lord.

Note: As a parent, you may decide when you want your child to participate in the sacrament of communion. When you are ready, discuss the meaning of the word and the sacrament with your child.

Community
(kuh-MYEW-nuh-tee)

EE: A group of people who meet together for a common purpose.

"Let us not give up meeting together, as some are in the habit of doing, but let us encourage one another—and all the more as you see the Day approaching," (Hebrews 10:25).

Think About It: Christians meet together to worship God and support one another. Who is someone that encourages you to live for God each day?

Compassion (kum-PA-shun)

ME/PT: Concern for others that leads to helping them.

*"This is what the LORD Almighty says: 'Administer true justice; show mercy and **compassion** to one another. Do not oppress the widow or the fatherless, the alien or the poor. In your hearts do not think evil of each other,'" (Zechariah 7:9-10).*

Think About It: Compassion is genuinely caring for others and doing something to help when they are in need. How do you show **compassion** for others through things that you do?

Condemn (kun-DEM)

PT: To say that something is wrong or to say that a person is guilty of wrongdoing and deserves punishment.

*"For God did not send his Son into the world to **condemn** the world, but to save the world through him," (John 3:17).*

Think About It: Jesus came so that we could be saved from sin instead of **condemned** by sin. How do you feel about Jesus' saving action?

Confess (kun-FES)

PT: To admit or acknowledge something. For example, to admit to God what you have done wrong. Or, to acknowledge that Christ is Lord.

*"If we **confess** our sins, he is faithful and just and will forgive us our sins and purify us from all unrighteousness," (1 John 1:9).*

Think About It: God is faithful. When we tell God if we do something wrong, and are truly sorry, He forgives us.

Consecrate (KAHN-see-KRAYT)

ME: To give yourself or something you have completely to God.

PT: To set apart an object or a person for God's use only.

*"'**Consecrate** yourselves and be holy, because I am the LORD your God. Keep my decrees and follow them. I am the LORD, who makes you holy,'" (Leviticus 20:7-8).*

Think About It: By giving yourself completely to God, you grow to be more Christlike. He is helping you to live a holy life, set apart for His work. What is something God might have you do for Him?

Convict (kun-VIKT)

PT: When the Holy Spirit causes us to realize our thoughts, words, or actions are sinful.

*"When he [Holy Spirit] comes, he will **convict** the world of guilt in regard to sin and righteousness and judgment," (John 16:8).*

Think About It: When you pray and listen for the Holy Spirit, He will help you know what is right and wrong. Do you stop and listen when you talk with God?

Conviction (kun-VIK-shun)

ME: A strong belief that guides a person's actions.

*"For we know, brothers loved by God, that he has chosen you, because our gospel came to you not simply with words, but also with power, with the Holy Spirit and with deep **conviction**. You know how we lived among you for your sake," (1 Thessalonians 1:4-5).*

Think About It: Why do you act the way that you do? What **conviction** or strong belief guides your choices? Is there anything that you do simply because you trust the person who tells you to do it? You can trust God to tell you to do what is right!

Covenant (KUV-uh-nunt)

ME/PT: An agreement between God and His people. Both God and people make promises to each other. God's **covenants** offer us a relationship of love with Him. A **covenant** is a binding contract.

*"Then I said: 'O Lord, God of heaven, the great and awesome God, who keeps his **covenant** of love with those who love him and obey his commands,'"* (Nehemiah 1:5).

Think About It: When you promise to love, obey, and serve God, then He promises to love you and make you His child. This is the most important **covenant** or promise you will ever make. Thank God for being a **covenant**-keeper.

Covet (KUV-it)

EE: To want very much what belongs to someone else. **Coveting** is a feeling that can lead people to disobey God.

ME/PT: To want something that belongs to someone else so much that a person is willing to disobey God to have it.

*"The commandments, 'Do not commit adultery,' 'Do not murder,' 'Do not steal,' 'Do not **covet**,' and whatever other commandment there may be, are summed up in this one rule: 'Love your neighbor as yourself,'"* (Romans 13:9).

Think About It: When you want what is best for someone else, it is difficult to want to hurt them or take something away from them. This is why loving others sums up God's command to "not **covet**."

Create (kree-AYT)

ME/PT: To make something new. God **created** the world and everything in it from nothing.

*"In the beginning God **created** the heavens and the earth," (Genesis 1:1).*

Think About It: Can you imagine what it was like when God **created** the world from nothing? What does it look like? Sound like? God is awesome!

Creator (kree-AY-ter)

EC: God is the **Creator**. In the beginning there was only God. Then God made everything!

EE: Someone who makes something new. God is the **Creator** of the heavens and the earth and everything in them.

ME/PT: A name for God, because He created the world and everything in it.

*"So then, those who suffer according to God's will should commit themselves to their faithful **Creator** and continue to do good," (1 Peter 4:19).*

Think About It: God is the **Creator**. He is faithful and unchanging. You can depend on God no matter what! Say a sentence prayer to the **Creator** of all things, thanking Him for His faithfulness.

Creed (KREED)

PT: A declaration of faith, such as the Apostles' **Creed**, often used in worship. **Creeds** summarize the most important Christian beliefs.

"But what does it say? 'The word is near you; it is in your mouth and in your heart,' that is, the word of faith we are proclaiming: That if you confess with your mouth, 'Jesus is Lord,' and believe in your heart that God raised him from the dead, you will be saved," (Romans 10:8-9).

Think About It: What is the most important thing that you believe to be true? How would you say it? For centuries, Christians have written down and said their most important beliefs, including the belief that Jesus is the Son of God. Ask someone to help you find the Apostles' **Creed** (page 139) and say it with you.

Cross (KRAHS)

ME: An object used long ago to execute criminals. Jesus died on a **cross** for the sins of the world, not for any crime that He committed. For Christians the **Cross** is a symbol of Jesus' death for sin.

*"For God was pleased to have all his fullness dwell in him, and through him to reconcile to himself all things, whether things on earth or things in heaven, by making peace through his blood, shed on the **cross**," (Colossians 1:19-20).*

Think About It: Jesus' death and resurrection is your hope for eternal life. How can you show others how important this truth is for them?

Note: Because of the connection with Easter, this word will be approached at early age levels. A simple explanation that this is the wood upon which Jesus died will be sufficient.

Crucifixion
(KREW-suh-FIK-shun)

EE: Death on a cross. **The Crucifixion** is when Jesus' enemies killed Him by nailing Him to the Cross.

*"He is not here; he has risen! Remember how he told you, while he was still with you in Galilee: 'The Son of Man must be delivered into the hands of sinful men, be **crucified** and on the third day be raised again,'" (Luke 24:6-7).*

Think About It: Good news! Jesus' **crucifixion** was not the end. It was a new hope! You can know Jesus, love and serve Him, because He is risen. Celebrate this new life by telling someone this Good News.

Note: Children will hear this word and may ask about it at this age and subsequent age levels. This is an explanation that will work for early elementary and older. For younger children, a simple answer, "This is about when Jesus died" will suffice.

Deity (DEE-uh-tee)

PT: This means god. Christians only use this word in reference to the one true God.

*"For in Christ all the fullness of the **Deity** lives in bodily form, and you have been given fullness in Christ, who is the head over every power and authority," (Colossians 2:9).*

Think About It: A wonderful thing about being a Christian is that in knowing Jesus Christ, we know God!

Disciple(s) (duh-SIE-pulz)

EE: People who love Jesus and obey His teachings. When Jesus was on earth, He chose 12 men to be His followers. These men were the first **disciples.**

ME: A person who follows the teachings and example of another person. All those who accept and follow Jesus are His **disciples**.

PT: A person who follows the teachings and example of another person. Jesus chose 12 **disciples** to help Him spread the gospel. Today all those who accept and follow Jesus are His **disciples**.

*"Therefore go and make **disciples** of all nations, baptizing them in the name of the Father and of the Son and of the Holy Spirit, and teaching them to obey everything I have commanded you. And surely I am with you always, to the very end of the age," (Matthew 28:19-20).*

Think About It: When we choose to follow Jesus, we become His **disciples**. Then we are called to go and make more **disciples**. How do you share Jesus with others?

Divine (duh-VIEN)

PT: Having the qualities of God.

*"His **divine** power has given us everything we need for life and godliness through our knowledge of him who called us by his own glory and goodness," (2 Peter 1:3).*

Think About It: God is with us and He helps us through the Holy Spirit to live lives that are completely pleasing to Him. Praise God for His love and guidance.

Easter (EE-ster)

EC: Easter is a special time when Christians celebrate that God's Son, Jesus, is alive.

"He is not here; he has risen, just as he said. Come and see the place where he lay. Then go quickly and tell his disciples: 'He has risen from the dead and is going ahead of you into Galilee. There you will see him.' Now I have told you," (Matthew 28:6-7).

Think About It: Share a favorite **Easter** memory. How did you celebrate that Jesus is alive?

Entire Sanctification
(EN-tier SANG-tuh-fuh-KAY-shun)

PT: An experience of God's grace that takes place after a person becomes a Christian. When we give ourselves completely to God, the Holy Spirit changes us so we want God's way more than our own way. As a result, Christians increasingly love God and other people. They find it easier to obey and serve God.

*"'**Sanctify** them by the truth; your word is truth. As you sent me into the world, I have sent them into the world. For them I **sanctify** myself, that they too may be truly **sanctified**,"* (John 17:17-19).

Think About It: Pray that God will help you want to be more like Him each day.

Eternal life (ee-TER-nul LIEF)

EE: Life with God that begins when we receive Jesus as Savior. It continues through life and forever with God in heaven.

ME/PT: The special kind of life God gives to those who trust Jesus as Savior. **Eternal life** is life as God's friend, which begins on earth. Those who keep trusting Jesus enjoy **eternal life** forever in heaven.

*"I tell you the truth, whoever hears my word and believes him who sent me has **eternal life** and will not be condemned; he has crossed over from death to life,"* (John 5:24).

Think About It: You have **eternal life** when Jesus is your Savior. Thank God for this gift.

Eternity (ee-TER-nuh-tee)

PT: Endless or immeasurable time. Christians will spend the rest of eternity with God.

*"Your throne was established long ago; you are from all **eternity**,"* (Psalm 93:2).

Think About It: God is immeasurable, eternal. He is without beginning or end. There is an immeasurable, unending time, **eternity**, that Christians will spend with God beyond life on this earth. How do you imagine this to be?

Eucharist (YEW-kuh-rust)

PT: This means to "give thanks." We celebrate this special meal (communion) together to show thanks to Jesus for dying for us. We also thank Him for leading us today.

"For whenever you eat this bread and drink this cup, you proclaim the Lord's death until he comes," (1 Corinthians 11:26).

Think About It: It is very important that when you celebrate the **Eucharist** together, that you are doing so as a follower of Christ. Do you know Christ as Lord and Savior?

Evangelism (ee-VAN-juh-liz-um)

PT: Presenting the good news of salvation through Jesus Christ to people who are not Christians.

"That is why I am so eager to preach the gospel also to you who are at Rome. I am not ashamed of the gospel, because it is the power of God for the salvation of everyone who believes: first for the Jew, then for the Gentile," (Romans 1:15-16).

Think About It: When we are saved and believe in Jesus, we are part of sharing salvation with others. That is **evangelism**. How do you share Jesus' love with people that you know?

Note: Children of all ages are natural evangelists. They share about Jesus with people they know and meet. They just do not know or understand the term evangelism.

Evangelist (ee-VAN-juh-list)

PT: A person who preaches about Jesus and tries to help people become Christians. In one sense, every Christian witness is an **evangelist**. However, God calls some people to full-time work as **evangelists**.

*"But you, keep your head in all situations, endure hardship, do the work of an **evangelist**, discharge all the duties of your ministry," (2 Timothy 4:5).*

Think About It: When you tell others about Jesus, you are an **evangelist**. **Evangelists** also are people who do the work of going and telling others about Jesus. Do you know any **evangelists**? Of course, it includes you!

Evil (EE-vuhl)

ME: Anything or anyone that is opposed to God. **Evil** is the opposite of good, and God is good.

PT: Anyone or anything that opposes God and His purposes in the world. Some **evil**, like sickness and death, is not sin. Sinful **evil** happens when people disobey God. This kind of **evil** damages our relationship with God.

*"To fear the LORD is to hate **evil**; I hate pride and arrogance, evil behavior and perverse speech," (Proverbs 8:13).*

Think About It: God is good. Thank God that you can choose to live for Him and not against Him.

Exodus (EK-suh-dus)

EE: "To leave." The **Exodus** was when God helped His people leave Egypt where they were slaves.

"Therefore, say to the Israelites: 'I am the LORD, and I will bring you out from under the yoke of the Egyptians. I will free you from being slaves to them, and I will redeem you with an outstretched arm and with mighty acts of judgment. I will take you as my own people, and I will be your God. Then you will know that I am the LORD your God, who brought you out from under the yoke of the Egyptians," (Exodus 6:6-7).

Think About It: God made a promise and He kept it with the **Exodus**. We can trust God to be with us, to help us, and to keep His promises.

Faith (FAYTH)

EE/ME: Believing God's Word and acting in a way that shows that belief. **Faith** is trust in action.

ME: Trust in God that leads people to believe what God has said, depend on Him, and obey Him.

PT: Believing God's Word and acting in a way that shows that belief. **Faith** is trust in action. **Faith** is necessary for salvation.

PT, expanded: Believing God's Word and acting in a way that shows that belief. **Faith** is trust in action. **Faith** is necessary for salvation. **Faith** can also be a doctrine or set of religious truths a person believes and to which he or she is loyal.

*"Now **faith** is being sure of what we hope for and certain of what we do not see,"* (Hebrews 11:1).

Think About It: What are some of your actions that show your **faith** in God's promises?

Faithful (FAYTH-ful)

EE: A **faithful** person can be trusted to keep promises. God is **faithful**. God expects His people to be **faithful** to Him and to others.

ME: Dependable and trustworthy. God is always **faithful**. We can trust Him to keep His promises. God expects His people to be **faithful** to Him and to others.

PT: Dependable, trustworthy, and loyal. God is **faithful**.

*"The one who calls you is **faithful** and he will do it,"* (1 Thessalonians 5:24).

Think About It: God is **faithful**. This means we can depend on Him. What are some ways that you depend on God?

Fall (FAWL)

PT: The separation of God and humanity that happened when Adam and Eve first disobeyed God. They no longer had a right relationship with God, and all creation was harmed.

*"For all have sinned and **fall** short of the glory of God," (Romans 3:23).*

Think About It: We live **fallen** or separated from God if we choose to sin. What must you do if you sin and disobey God?

Family of God (FAM-uh-lee of GAHD)

PT: All Christians who are born again and believe in God are adopted into His family. Christians become children of God.

"The Spirit himself testifies with our spirit that we are God's children. Now if we are children, then we are heirs—heirs of God and co-heirs with Christ, if indeed we share in his sufferings in order that we may also share in his glory," (Romans 8:16-17).

Think About It: As God's children we are a part of His family. What is your favorite part of being a part of the **family of God**?

Fast (FAST)

ME: To give up something for a time, usually food, in order to pray and focus on God.

*"But when you **fast**, put oil on your head and wash your face, so that it will not be obvious to men that you are **fasting**, but only to your Father, who is unseen; and your Father, who sees what is done in secret, will reward you," (Matthew 6:17-18).*

Think About It: Choosing to **fast** is something between you and God. It is for focusing on Him. What are some ways that you keep your focus on God?

Fear (FEER)

ME: To have deep respect and reverence for God, which includes a strong desire not to offend Him.

*"Serve the LORD with **fear** and rejoice with trembling," (Psalm 2:11).*

Think About It: How can you show a deep respect or **fear** for God's awesome power and authority through your words and actions?

Fellowship (FEL-oh-ship)

PT: Love, care, and companionship that result from having something in common. Christian **fellowship** grows out of a shared belief in Christ. Christians also have **fellowship** with God the Father, Son, and Holy Spirit.

*"But if we walk in the light, as he is in the light, we have **fellowship** with one another, and the blood of Jesus, his Son, purifies us from all sin," (1 John 1:7).*

Think About It: How do you have **fellowship** with other Christians, family, and friends?

Follower of Jesus
(FAH-luh-wer of JEE-zus)

EC: A **follower of Jesus** is someone who loves Jesus and tells others about Him. Peter was a **follower of Jesus.**

EE: Someone who believes that Jesus is God's Son. A **follower of Jesus** loves and obeys Him.

*"Whoever serves me must **follow** me; and where I am, my servant also will be. My Father will honor the one who serves me,"* (John 12:26).

Think About It: A **follower of Jesus** does as He does. How do you show others that you are like Jesus?

Fool (FEWL)

PT: A person who lacks good sense and wisdom. Those who reject God and His ways are **fools**.

*"He who trusts in himself is a **fool**, but he who walks in wisdom is kept safe,"* (Proverbs 28:26).

Think About It: True wisdom or the smarts to make the right choices come from God. It is a **fool** who thinks he or she knows better than God.

Forgive (fohr-GIV)

ME/PT: To pardon someone who has done wrong and stop being angry with him or her.

*"For if you **forgive** men when they sin against you, your heavenly Father will also **forgive** you,"* (Matthew 6:14).

Think About It: When you know God's **forgiveness**, it becomes a part of who you are to **forgive** others who hurt you. Is there someone that you need to **forgive**?

Forgiveness (fohr-GIV-nus)

ME/PT: The act of pardoning a person who has done wrong.

*"In him we have redemption through his blood, the **forgiveness** of sins, in accordance with the riches of God's grace that he lavished on us with all wisdom and understanding," (Ephesians 1:7-8).*

Think About It: Jesus' death is **forgiveness** in action for all people, and that includes you! Thank God for the **forgiveness** that you are freely given.

Free will (FREE WIL)

PT: The God-given ability and freedom to make choices. Human beings have **free will** because they are made in the image of God and because of God's grace.

*"It is for **freedom** that Christ has set us **free**. Stand firm, then, and do not let yourselves be burdened again by a yoke of slavery," (Galatians 5:1).*

Think About It: Free will means you get a choice. Have you chosen to follow God?

Friend (FREND)

EC: Someone whom you enjoy being with and know well. Jesus becomes our best Friend when we choose to believe in Him.

*"You are my **friends** if you do what I command. I no longer call you servants, because a servant does not know his master's business. Instead, I have called you **friends**, for everything that I learned from my Father I have made known to you, (John 15:14-15).*

Think About It: Who is your closest **friend**? Someone that you tell everything to? This is what Jesus is. He is closer than even your very closest **friend**.

Fruit of the Spirit (FREWT of the SPIR-it)

PT: Christian virtues. Read Galatians 5:22-23. The Christian grows to be like Jesus with the help of the Holy Spirit.

*"But the **fruit of the Spirit** is love, joy, peace, patience, kindness, goodness, faithfulness, gentleness and self-control. Against such things there is no law," (Galatians 5:22-23).*

Think About It: When you live for God, God lives in you. The **fruit of the Spirit** are traits that you show. Are you loving, joyful, peaceful, patient, kind, good, faithful, gentle, and self-controlled? This is God at work changing you!

Gentile (JEN-tiel)

ME: Any person who is not a Jew.

*"And now the LORD says—he who formed me in the womb to be his servant to bring Jacob back to him and gather Israel to himself, for I am honored in the eyes of the LORD and my God has been my strength— he says: 'It is too small a thing for you to be my servant to restore the tribes of Jacob and bring back those of Israel I have kept. I will also make you a light for the **Gentiles**, that you may bring my salvation to the ends of the earth,'" (Isaiah 49:5-6).*

Think About It: God's plan for all people is to come to know Him. Jews and **Gentiles**. That includes you!

Glorify (GLOH-ruh-fie)

PT: To bring honor or praise to someone or something.

*"**Glorify** the LORD with me; let us exalt his name together," (Psalm 34:3).*

Think About It: You are made to praise God. Who you are and everything you do and say should **glorify** or honor Him.

God (GAHD)

EC: God, the Creator of all things, shows His love for us in many ways.

EE: God is our Heavenly Father, who created us and loves us.

ME: The Creator of everything, and the Ruler of the universe. He has always lived and always will live. He is not limited in any way. One way we know **God** is as our Heavenly Father.

PT: We know God as Lord. He is the one true God. God is triune. He is one God who reveals himself in three persons. He is God the Father, Jesus Christ the Son, and the Holy Spirit.

*"Love the LORD your **God** and keep his requirements, his decrees, his laws and his commands always," (Deuteronomy 11:1).*

Think About It: When you know and love **God,** you choose to obey Him. How are you obedient to **God** each day?

Godliness (GAHD-lee-nus)

PT: A way of being, thinking, and acting that honors God

*"For physical training is of some value, but **godliness** has value for all things, holding promise for both the present life and the life to come," (1 Timothy 4:8).*

Think About It: You know that everything you do and say can honor or dishonor God, but your thoughts can also honor God. What are godly thoughts?

God's care (GAHD's KAIR)

EC: God's care is what God does that shows He loves us and wants us to have what we need.

*"O LORD, what is man that you **care** for him, the son of man that you think of him?" (Psalm 144:3).*

Think About It: Tell about a time in your family that you experienced **God's care** for your needs.

God's help (GAHD's HELP)

EC: **God's help** means the things that God does to care for us and help us know what He wants us to do.

*"God is our refuge and strength, an ever-present **help** in trouble," (Psalm 46:1).*

Think About It: God is with us. You can count on Him for help in good times and bad. How do you see **God's help** in your everyday life?

God's power (GAHD's POW-er)

EC: God is great. God is **powerful**.

EE: **God's power** is greater and stronger than anyone or anything. God can do all things.

ME: **Power** that is greater and stronger than anyone or anything. God can do all things.

PT: **Power** that is greater and stronger than anyone or anything. God can do all things. People can trust that **God** uses His **power** to care for the world and people.

*"Great is our Lord and mighty in **power**; his understanding has no limit," (Psalm 147:5).*

Think About It: How do you feel when you think about **God's power** available for you? What do you picture when you think about **all-powerful God**?

God's will (GAHD's WIL)

ME: What God wants for all of His creation. The Holy Spirit reveals **God's will** to us as we pray, read the Bible, and talk with experienced Christians.

*"I desire to do **your will**, O my God; your law is within my heart," (Psalm 40:8).*

Think About It: When God is Lord of all, you want to live within **His will**. This means you follow **God's will** for the choices that you make. What choices has God helped you to make?

God's work (GAHD's WERK)

EE/ME: Everything that God does. **God's work** is also anything God asks people to do.

*"In all my prayers for all of you, I always pray with joy because of your partnership in the gospel from the first day until now, being confident of this, that he who began a good **work** in you will carry it on to completion until the day of Christ Jesus," (Philippians 1:4-6).*

Think About It: How does God **work** in you and through you to help others?

Note: There are times that two age levels are presented together. This simply means that depending upon the development of your child; you can introduce a word successfully with the given definition at either age.

Golden Rule
(GOHL-dun REWL)

ME: Jesus teaches the Golden Rule. See Matthew 7:12 and Luke 6:31. It simply teaches us to "do to others what you would have them do to you." This means we should treat others with care, compassion, and respect.

"So in everything, do to others what you would have them do to you, for this sums up the Law and the Prophets," (Matthew 7:12).

Think About It: How do you want other people to treat you? That is how God expects you to treat them. Be kind today!

Good Friday (GOOD FRI-day)

EC: The Friday before Easter Sunday. This is the day that Christians remember that Jesus died on the Cross.

"This man was handed over to you by God's set purpose and foreknowledge; and you, with the help of wicked men, put him to death by nailing him to the cross," (Acts 2:23).

Think About It: This Good Friday think about how difficult it must have been for Jesus to die for you, but He still did it! How can you thank Jesus for His sacrifice?

Good News (GOOD NEWZ)

EC: God loves us and sent His Son, Jesus. This is the **Good News** that Christians tell others.

"Whoever has my commands and obeys them, he is the one who loves me. He who loves me will be loved by my Father, and I too will love him and show myself to him," John 14:21).

Think About It: Tell someone of God's love. Share the **Good News**!

Gospel (GAHS-pul)

ME/PT: The good news that Jesus Christ died for our sins and rose from the dead. Therefore forgiveness and freedom from sin's power are available to all people.

*"However, I consider my life worth nothing to me, if only I may finish the race and complete the task the Lord Jesus has given me—the task of testifying to the **gospel** of God's grace,"* (Acts 20:24).

Think About It: How can you share Jesus' love with people you know and people that you do not know?

Grace (GRAYS)

ME/PT: God's love, mercy, forgiveness, and power at work in our lives. God freely gives us His **grace** because He loves us, not because we deserve it.

*"The law was added so that the trespass might increase. But where sin increased, **grace** increased all the more,"* (Romans 5:20).

Think About It: There is nothing greater than the **grace** of God. It is not something that is earned. It is a gift. What was the best gift you ever received? This gift is even greater!

Gracious (GRAY shus)

ME: To treat someone with kindness, compassion, and forgiveness. To share what one has to help others.

*"They refused to listen and failed to remember the miracles you performed among them. They became stiff-necked and in their rebellion appointed a leader in order to return to their slavery. But you are a forgiving God, **gracious** and compassionate, slow to anger and abounding in love. Therefore you did not desert them,"* (Nehemiah 9:17).

Think About It: Because God is gracious to you, you can be **gracious** to others. Is there anyone you need to forgive or show kindness to?

Growth in grace (GROHTH in GRAYS)

PT: The spiritual growth that happens as the Holy Spirit leads a believer to learn more about God, love Him more, and live in His way.

"And in him you too are being built together to become a dwelling in which God lives by his Spirit," (Ephesians 2:22).

Think About It: How has God helped you to change your actions, words, thoughts, and choices as you grow in Him?

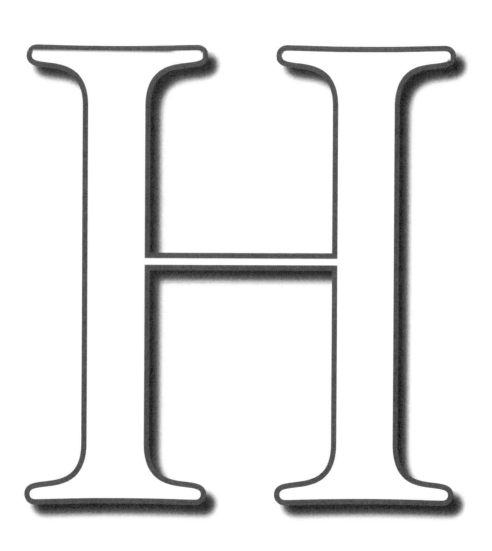

75

Hallowed (HΛL oh-ed)

ME: People or things that are honored and revered because they are holy.

*"This, then, is how you should pray: 'Our Father in heaven, **hallowed** be your name, your kingdom come, your will be done on earth as it is in heaven. Give us today our daily bread. Forgive us our debts, as we also have forgiven our debtors. And lead us not into temptation, but deliver us from the evil one. Amen,'" (Matthew 6:9-13).*

Think About It: Hallowed means "holy" and appears in the Bible within The Lord's Prayer. You may have learned this prayer using trespasses instead of debts. Do you ever recite this prayer as a part of a church service? Many people do so. Learn this with your family. Talk about how Jesus used this to teach His disciples how to pray. 1) Acknowledge God as Lord and your desire to do His will. 2) State your petitions or need for God's work in your life, knowing that God hears and answers prayer. 3) Ask for and receive God's forgiveness. 4) Admit your need to forgive others. Then forgive! 5) Ask for God's help in avoiding and overcoming temptation to sin against Him and His will for your life. 6) Seek God's protection from the devil and his evil influence. 7) Close the prayer, acknowledging that God will do His work in your life as you have sought from Him.

Heart (HAHRT)

ME: A person's inner being. The heart is where our thoughts, feelings, desires, character, and choices come from.

*"For it is with your **heart** that you believe and are justified, and it is with your mouth that you confess and are saved," (Romans 10:10).*

Think About It: Look inside your **heart**. Do you love God with everything that you are and everything that you have? What does this look like in how you live, think, and feel?

Heaven (HEV-un)

EE/ME: The home of God and His angels. It is where God's will is done completely. Believers will go to **heaven** some day and live forever with God. Even now, Christians are "citizens of **heaven**" because God is part of our lives.

*"But our citizenship is in **heaven**. And we eagerly await a Savior from there, the Lord Jesus Christ, who, by the power that enables him to bring everything under his control, will transform our lowly bodies so that they will be like his glorious body," (Philippians 3:20-21).*

Think About It: What do you think **heaven** will be like? Describe it to another person.

High Priest (HIE PREEST)

PT: The most important priest in Bible times. The **high priest** offered the sacrifice on the Day of Atonement. Moses' brother, Aaron, was the first **high priest.** Now, our **high priest** is Christ.

*"Therefore, since we have a great **high priest** who has gone through the heavens, Jesus the Son of God, let us hold firmly to the faith we profess," (Hebrews 4:14).*

Think About It: Jesus knows us. He loves us. He talks to God the Father for us. Thank God for Jesus, your **high priest**. Tell Him your deepest need.

Holiness (HOH-lee-nus)

PT: Being like God in righteousness and moral purity. God cleanses us and helps us live holy lives after we give ourselves completely to Him.

*"You were taught, with regard to your former way of life, to put off your old self, which is being corrupted by its deceitful desires; to be made new in the attitude of your minds; and to put on the new self, created to be like God in true righteousness and **holiness**," (Ephesians 4:22-24).*

Think About It: How does God change the choices that you make? Your attitude toward others? Pray each day to be made more like Him.

Holy (HOH-lee)

ME: To be perfect, complete and pure, or to be set apart for God's use only God is **holy**. He is different from all other beings, and everything about Him is good and perfect.

PT: To be perfect, complete, and pure, or to be set apart for God's use only. God is **holy** because He is different from all other beings and everything about Him is good and perfect. People begin to be **holy** (like God) when God saves them and gives them His Spirit. **Holy** also describes things that Christians belong to God and are set apart for His purposes.

*"Exalt the LORD our God and worship at his **holy** mountain, for the LORD our God is **holy**," (Psalm 99:9).*

Think About It: The word "**holy**" is used many times throughout the Scripture. How many times can you find? This is an important word. Why do you think it is important to know and understand?

Holy Spirit (HOH-lee SPIR-ut)

ME: The Spirit of God. We receive the **Holy Spirit** when we trust Jesus as Savior. The **Holy Spirit** then helps us live for God.

PT: The Spirit of God, the third person of the Trinity. The **Holy Spirit** changes our hearts and empowers us to live for God as we trust Jesus as Savior.

*"You will receive power when the **Holy Spirit** comes on you; and you will be my witnesses in Jerusalem, and in all Judea and Samaria, and to the ends of the earth," (Acts 1:8).*

Think About It: How does God help you through the **Holy Spirit**? Ask this question of yourself and your family members.

Honor (ON-er)

EE: To show how great God is. We **honor** God when we say good things about Him. We also honor God when we love and obey Him.

ME/PT: To show how great someone is or to show respect for a person. We **honor** God when we praise Him, and love and obey Him.

*"You are worthy, our Lord and God, to receive glory and **honor** and power, for you created all things, and by your will they were created and have their being,"* (Revelation 4:11).

Think About It: It is time to make a list! List everything good about God, and then praise Him for who He is and all He is to you.

Hope (HOHP)

ME: A feeling of certainty that God will keep His promises. **Hope** grows out of trust in God.

PT: A feeling of certainty that God will keep His promises. **Hope** grows out of trust in God and helps us be joyful even in difficult times.

*"A faith and knowledge resting on the **hope** of eternal life, which God, who does not lie, promised before the beginning of time,"* (Titus 1:2).

Think About It: We have **hope** that God is with us now and forever when we choose to love, serve, and follow Him. God does not lie. God keeps His promises. This is a foundation for real **hope**. Thank God for His forever faithfulness.

Hypocrisy (hi-PAHK-ruh-see)

PT: To live a lie. To claim to believe something that you do not believe. To deceive others through your words and actions. A hypocrite would claim to believe in God, but not really believe.

*"Therefore, rid yourselves of all malice and all deceit, **hypocrisy**, envy, and slander of every kind,"* (1 Peter 2:1).

Think About It: What is the opposite of **hypocrisy**? That's right! You would be honest with God, yourself, and others! How can you live honestly?

Idol (IE-dul)

ME: Anything that is worshiped instead of God or loved more than God.

*"You shall have no other gods before me. You shall not make for yourself an **idol** in the form of anything in heaven above or on the earth beneath or in the waters below,"* *(Exodus 20:3-4).*

Think About It: What is important to you? Think about these people or things. Is God the most important to you, before anyone or anything else? How does this show in your life and the choices that you make?

Image of God (IM-ij of GAHD)

ME: Characteristics people share with God. Only people were created in the **image of God**.

PT: Characteristics people share with God. Only people were created in the **image of God**. This allows us to fellowship with God.

*"When God created man, he made him in the **likeness of God**,"* *(Genesis 5:1).*

Think About It: You are made in **God's likeness or image**. You can live and love and become more like Him. Praise God for this special gift!

Immanuel (i-MAN-yuh-wul)

ME/PT: A Hebrew word that means "God with us." This name is given to Jesus in the Bible.

*"Therefore the Lord himself will give you a sign: The virgin will be with child and will give birth to a son, and will call him **Immanuel**," (Isaiah 7:14).*

Think About It: How do you know that Jesus is with you each day?

Incarnation (IN-kahr-NAY-shun)

PT: The event in which God's Son became a human being, Jesus Christ. He became fully human, yet remained fully God.

"The Word became flesh and made his dwelling among us. We have seen his glory, the glory of the One and Only, who came from the Father, full of grace and truth," (John 1:14).

Think About It: This verse describes for us who Jesus is. He is the Son of God. We can know, love, and serve Him. What is one thing you do to serve Him?

Inspiration (IN-spuh-RAY-shun)

ME: The way in which God—through the Holy Spirit—guided human authors to write His Word. Because the Bible is inspired, its message is true.

*"All Scripture is **God-breathed** and is useful for teaching, rebuking, correcting and training in righteousness, so that the man of God may be thoroughly equipped for every good work," (2 Timothy 3:16-17).*

Think About It: God-breathed is used to describe how God **inspired** the writers of the Bible. This means we can trust the Bible to be true. What is your favorite Bible verse or story? Tell it to someone.

Intercede (IN-ter-SEED)

PT: To present the needs or interests of one person to another person. To help one person better understand another person. To pray for another person's needs. In heaven, Jesus **intercedes** for us with God the Father.

*"Because Jesus lives forever, he has a permanent priesthood. Therefore he is able to save completely those who come to God through him, because he always lives to **intercede** for them," (Hebrews 7:24-25).*

Think About It: It is terrific to know Jesus speaks on our behalf! And God listens! We can pray with confidence knowing this truth. Think of three things you would like to pray about. Now pray for them.

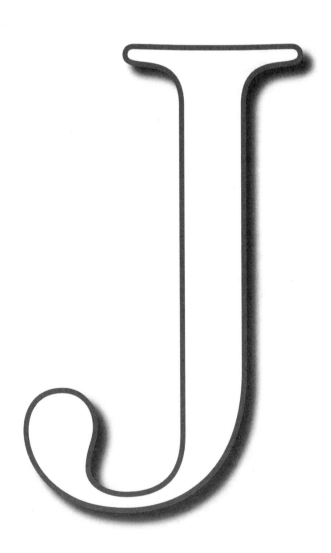

Jealousy (JEL-uh-see)

ME: Feelings of envy, dislike, or hostility toward someone who has something you want.

*"Anger is cruel and fury overwhelming, but who can stand before **jealousy**? (Proverbs 27:4).*

Think About It: Untamed **jealousy** is harmful to you. It is emotionally hurtful and it harms your relationship with God. What can you do if you feel **jealousy**?

Jesus (JEE-zus)

EC/EE: Jesus is God's Son. He came to earth to show us God's love. He teaches us many things. We can choose to love and follow Jesus.

ME: God's only Son, the Savior of the world. **Jesus** is fully God and fully human.

PT: God's only Son, the Second Person of the Trinity, the Savior of the world. **Jesus** is fully God and fully human.

"For God so loved the world that he gave his one and only Son, that whoever believes in him shall not perish but have eternal life," (John 3:16).

Think About It: Who is God's only Son? How has knowing and loving **Jesus** changed you? Do you need to accept **Jesus** as Savior? If yes, talk to someone that you know and trust to help you do so.

Joy (JOY)

PT: A feeling of deep happiness and satisfaction. Christian joy is based on a relationship of love and trust in God regardless of outward circumstances.

"May the God of hope fill you with all joy and peace as you trust in him, so that you may overflow with hope by the power of the Holy Spirit," (Romans 15:13).

Think About It: Think of a time when you felt amazing **joy**. What made this so joyful? **Joy** in God is about more than that! You can have great **joy** no matter what because you know God's love. Praise God with **joy**.

Judge (JUJ)

ME/PT: (verb) To form an opinion or make a decision. Jesus warns us against **judging** unfairly or making a quick decision without listening to all sides. He also teaches us to look at ourselves before we criticize the actions of others.

ME/PT: (noun) A person in the Old Testament chosen by God to rescue the Israelites from their enemies and lead them in obeying God. A military leader with power to make laws and enforce them.

"He will judge the world in righteousness; he will govern the peoples with justice," (Psalm 9:8).

Think About It: God is the ultimate and only truly righteous and fair **judge**. Ask God to help you be fair and loving when **judging** the actions of others.

Judgment (JUJ-munt)

PT: A conclusion about someone's character, motives, thoughts, and actions. Only God can make a final judgment about these things and whether a person goes to heaven or hell.

*"The LORD reigns forever; he has established his throne for **judgment**,"* (Psalm 9:7).

Think About It: A judge sits in **judgment**. This should be God. You can trust God to judge you because He created you and knows you better than anyone else.

Justification (JUS-tuh-fuh-KAY-shun)

PT: God's action to forgive sinners who repent, free them from guilt and punishment for their sins, and make them right with Him. After a person is **justified,** God no longer holds that person's sin against him or her.

*"Know that a man is not **justified** by observing the law, but by faith in Jesus Christ. So we, too, have put our faith in Christ Jesus that we may be **justified** by faith in Christ and not by observing the law, because by observing the law no one will be **justified**,"* (Galatians 2:16).

Think About It: Thank God for His **justifying** power in your life through belief in and obedience to Jesus. You can have faith that He forgives your sins. That is good news!

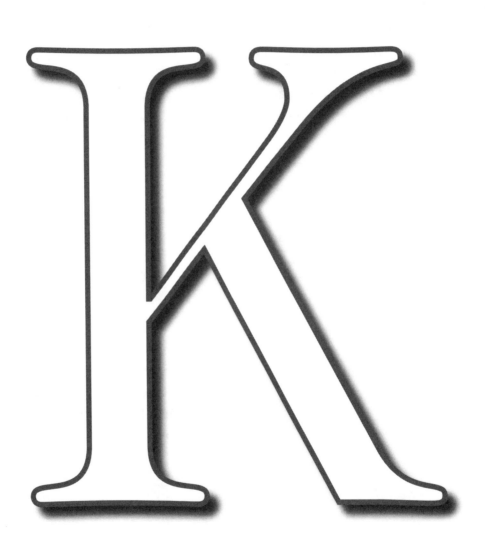

Kingdom of God
(KING-dum of GAHD)

EE: Wherever God rules. God has power over everything, but only those who obey God are part of His **kingdom**.

ME: Wherever God rules. We see **God's Kingdom** best where people worship and obey Him as Lord of their lives.

PT: Wherever God rules, especially in the lives of his people. Only those who obey God are part of His **kingdom**. **God's kingdom** will be complete after Jesus returns.

*"'The time has come,' he said. 'The **kingdom of God** is near. Repent and believe the good news!'" (Mark 1:15).*

Think About It: Those who love, serve, and obey God are a part of His **kingdom**. Are you a part? How do you live like someone in **God's kingdom**?

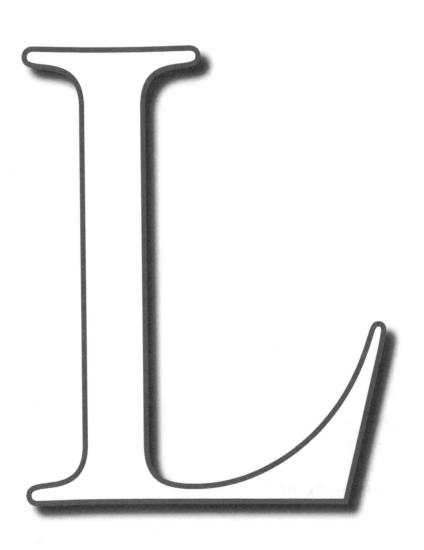

Law (LAW)

PT: The rules God gave to Moses, to teach Israel to be holy. These rules are found in the first five books of the Old Testament. The first five books are known as the Pentateuch or Torah. Pentateuch means five. Torah means law or teaching.

*"Do not think that I have come to abolish the **Law** or the Prophets; I have not come to abolish them but to fulfill them," (Matthew 5:17).*

Think About It: God wants your obedience! He wants you to love Him first, and then love others. Jesus said that this is what the **Law** is all about—loving God and loving others.

Lord's Prayer (LOHRDZ PRAYR)

ME: This is the prayer that Jesus taught His disciples to pray. See Matthew 6:9-13 and Luke 11:2-4. Christians still use this as a model of how to pray. Christians pray this prayer.

"He [Jesus] said to them, 'When you pray, say: 'Father, hallowed be your name, your kingdom come. Give us each day our daily bread. Forgive us our sins, for we also forgive everyone who sins against us. And lead us not into temptation,'" (Luke 11:2-4).

Think About It: The Lord's Prayer is how you are to pray. Jesus taught it to His disciples. He taught it for you too! Look up this prayer in Matthew and Luke. Pray it this week. Ask God to help you trust in Him.

Lord's Supper
(LOHRDZ SUP-er)

PT: This reminds us of Jesus last supper or meal with His disciples before His death. Jesus told His disciples they were to continue this special meal after His death. Many Christians do this today when they participate in the Sacrament of communion.

"And he [Jesus] took bread, gave thanks and broke it, and gave it to them, saying, 'This is my body given for you; do this in remembrance of me.' In the same way, after the supper he took the cup, saying, 'This cup is the new covenant in my blood, which is poured out for you,'" (Luke 22:19-20).

Think About It: Today you may participate in communion. This is also called **The Lord's Supper**. It is a way we remember what Jesus did for people on the Cross. It is also a way that you can participate in the new life that Jesus has provided you!

Love (LUV)

EC: Caring very much for others. God **loves** everyone.

EE: To care about other people and want what is best for them. We can trust in God's **love** for us and that He wants what is best for us.

ME: To care about other people, want what is best for them, and do good to them. God helps Christians to **love** even those who do not **love** them in return.

PT: To care about other people, want what is best for them, and do good to them. **Love** also includes a bond of loyalty among those in covenant with God. God helps Christians to **love** even those who do not **love** them in return.

*"How great is the **love** the Father has lavished on us, that we should be called children of God! And that is what we are! The reason the world does not know us is that it did not know him," (1 John 3:1).*

Think About It: Name three people that you **love**. Show these people God's **love** this week. You can show God's **love** because you know and experience His great **love** for you!

Mediator (MEE-dee-AY-ter)

PT: One who helps bring about peace or agreement between two other people or groups, by working with both groups. A **mediator** cares about the interests of both groups. Jesus is our **mediator** to God the Father.

*"For this reason Christ is the **mediator** of a new covenant, that those who are called may receive the promised eternal inheritance—now that he has died as a ransom to set them free from the sins committed under the first covenant,"* (Hebrews 9:15).

Think About It: Can you think of someone in your life who speaks to others for you in order to help you? That is what Jesus does for you with God. You can pray knowing that Jesus is there speaking to God for you!

Meek (MEEK)

PT: People who are humble before God and patient and gentle with other people.

*"Blessed are the **meek**, for they will inherit the earth,"* (Matthew 5:5).

Think About It: How would you describe being **meek** to another person? Do you know someone who is **meek** before God and with others? What is special about that person?

Mercy (MER-see)

ME: Forgiveness or kindness to a wrongdoer.

PT: Canceling or reducing the punishment someone deserves, or offering forgiveness.

*"Remember, O LORD, your great **mercy** and love, for they are from of old,"* (Psalm 25:6).

Think About It: One of the defining characteristics of God, who He is, is that He is **merciful** and loving. This is unchanging. We can depend upon His loving **mercy**.

Messiah (muh-SIE-uh)

ME: The "anointed one," sent by God to do His will. Jesus is the **Messiah**.

*"The woman said, 'I know that **Messiah'** (called Christ) 'is coming. When he comes, he will explain everything to us.'*

Then Jesus declared, 'I who speak to you am he,'" (John 4:25-26).

Think About It: Jesus affirmed that He is the **Messiah**. Only Jesus can claim this title, because He is the only Son of God. Give thanks to God for sending Jesus, the **Messiah**, to save you from your sins.

Miracle (MIR-uh-kul)

EC: Is something special that Jesus can do because He is God's Son.

EE: An amazing happening that shows God's power. You can't explain what happened in any other way.

ME/PT: An amazing act that God does to help people. God's **miracles** show people His character and power, and help them trust Him.

*"'But if I do it, even though you do not believe me, believe the **miracles**, that you may know and understand that the Father is in me, and I in the Father,'" (John 10:38).*

Think About It: Jesus spoke these words to people who did not believe in Him. We can see Jesus' **miracles** and choose to believe that He is the Son of God. Do you believe in, love, and serve Jesus?

Missionary (MISH-uh-NAIR-ee)

ME/PT: A person called by God and sent by the Church to take the gospel to people of other countries or cultures.

"While they were worshiping the Lord and fasting, the Holy Spirit said, 'Set apart for me Barnabas and Saul for the work to which I have called them.' So after they had fasted and prayed, they placed their hands on them and sent them off," (Acts 13:2-3).

Think About It: Who are the two **missionaries** named in this scripture? What is something that you know **missionaries** do today?

Missions (MISH-uns)

PT: To share the good news of Jesus Christ with another culture in all areas of life and throughout the world, either at home or in a different place.

"'Men, why are you doing this? We too are only men, human like you. We are bringing you good news, telling you to turn from these worthless things to the living God, who made heaven and earth and sea and everything in them,'" (Acts 14:15).

Think About It: You can be involved in **missions** at home. How do you bring the good news of salvation through Jesus Christ to people that you know and people that you meet?

Mourn (MORN)

PT: To feel deep sorrow for one's own sins, and for all the sin and evil in the world.

*"Blessed are those who **mourn**, for they will be comforted," (Matthew 5:4).*

Think About It: This verse promises comfort when you **mourn**. So if you are deeply and truly sorry for your sins, you can trust in God to forgive you.

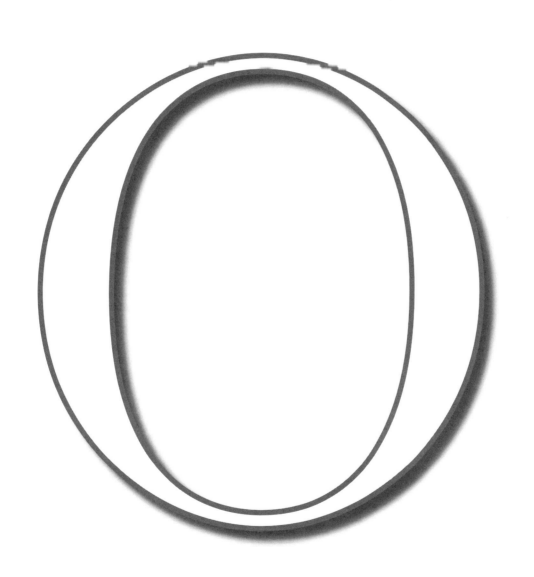

Obedience (oh-BEE-dee-uns)

ME: To do what someone tells you to do. God wants us to obey Him. When we choose to obey God, we are choosing to be obedient.

*"Through him and for his name's sake, we received grace and apostleship to call people from among all the Gentiles to the **obedience** that comes from faith. And you also are among those who are called to belong to Jesus Christ," (Romans 1:5-6).*

Think About It: When you belong to God, you choose **obedience** to Him. How are you **obedient** to God in the way that you live and the choices that you make?

Obey (oh-BAY)

EC: To **obey** is to do what God says we should do.

EE: To do what someone tells you to do. God wants us to **obey** Him.

ME: To do what God wants us to do. God wants us to **obey** (do) what He tells us in the Bible.

ME/PT: To do what someone tells you to do. God wants us to **obey** Him. Obeying God shows that we love Him.

*"Now if you **obey** me fully and keep my covenant, then out of all nations you will be my treasured possession," (Exodus 19:5).*

Think About It: When you **obey** God, you show Him love. What are some ways that you have shown God love by **obeying** Him today?

Offering (AWF-er-ing)

EC: A gift from people to God.

EE/ME: A gift from people to God. An **offering** can be obedience, time, money, or things we do.

*"Be imitators of God, therefore, as dearly loved children and live a life of love, just as Christ loved us and gave himself up for us as a fragrant **offering** and sacrifice to God," (Ephesians 5:1-2).*

Think About It: What do you think of when you hear the word, **offering**? Did you know that you can be an **offering**? It is true, your whole life can be an **offering** to God.

Original sin (uh-RIJ-uh-nul SIN)

PT: The first human disobedience to God, which has affected all people born since then. All people are born without a personal relationship with God and with a tendency to turn away from Him to their own way.

"They exchanged the truth of God for a lie, and worshiped and served created things rather than the Creator—who is forever praised. Amen," (Romans 1:25).

Think About It: All people are born without a personal relationship with God. There comes a time when you make a choice. You can choose to serve God, or you choose your own sinful and selfish way. What choice have you made or need to make?

Outreach (OUT-REECH)

ME: Any means of trying to reach people to win them to Christ.

"In everything set them an example by doing what is good. . . ," (Titus 2:7).

Think About It: Everything you do and say can be an **outreach** to others as people see Jesus lived out in your life. How do you show Jesus' love with words and actions?

Note: Talk with your child about how God calls all people to do this. It is known as the Great Commission and found in Matthew 28:19. These are the words of Jesus to His disciples.

Pagan (PAY-gun)

ME: Someone who does not believe in the Christian God. Some **pagans** worship many gods. Others don't worship any god.

*"You know that when you were **pagans**, somehow or other you were influenced and led astray to mute idols," (1 Corinthians 12:2).*

Think About It: If you are a **pagan**, you do not know or believe in God. How does that sound to you? It sounds horribly lonely to me!

Palm Sunday (PAHM SUN-dee)

PK: The Sunday before Easter. **Palm Sunday** celebrates Jesus' triumphal entry into Jerusalem when people used palm branches and other things to worship Him.

"A very large crowd spread their cloaks on the road, while others cut branches from the trees and spread them on the road.

The crowds that went ahead of him and those that followed shouted, 'Hosanna to the Son of David!' 'Blessed is he who comes in the name of the Lord!' 'Hosanna in the highest!'" (Matthew 21:8-9).

Think About It: This was the very first **Palm Sunday**. The crowds celebrated as Jesus entered Jerusalem, but what happened soon after? That's right, Jesus was crucified. But that is not the end of the story. It is just the beginning. What good news do we now celebrate, knowing that Jesus is alive?

Parable(s) (PAIR-uh-buls)

EC: Parables are special stories Jesus told.

EE: A special story Jesus told to teach something important about God.

ME: A short story that uses familiar things to teach a special lesson.

PT: A short story that uses familiar things to teach a special lesson. Jesus used **parables** to explain something about God or His kingdom.

*"Jesus spoke all these things to the crowd in **parables**; he did not say anything to them without using a **parable**. So was fulfilled what was spoken through the prophet: 'I will open my mouth in **parables**, I will utter things hidden since the creation of the world,'" (Matthew 13:34-35).*

Think About It: What is a favorite **parable** that Jesus told? What did it teach you?

Pardon (PAHR-dun)

ME: To forgive or excuse someone, or to release the person from punishment.

*"Seek the LORD while he may be found; call on him while he is near. Let the wicked forsake his way and the evil man his thoughts. Let him turn to the LORD, and he will have mercy on him, and to our God, for he will freely **pardon**," (Isaiah 55:6-7).*

Think About It: Only God can give you free and complete **pardon**. Have you asked God for forgiveness of your sins? Would you like to? Talk with someone that you trust.

Passover (PAS-OH-ver)

EE/ME: The annual Jewish feast that celebrates God's deliverance of the Israelites from slavery in Egypt.

PT: The annual Jewish feast that celebrates God's deliverance of the Israelites from slavery in Egypt. It is called **Passover** because God struck the firstborn of Egyptian families dead but "passed over" the firstborn in Jewish households.

*"So Moses told the Israelites to celebrate the **Passover**, and they did so in the Desert of Sinai at twilight on the fourteenth day of the first month. The Israelites did everything just as the LORD commanded Moses,"* (Numbers 9:4-5).

Think About It: It is important to celebrate what God has done for you. The celebration of the **Passover** was one thing the Jewish people did to remember what God had done in Egypt to free them from slavery. What are some important celebrations that show thankfulness for what God has done for you?

Pastor (PAS-ter)

EE: This is the minister who leads the congregation of people in a local church. This word is from the Greek that means "shepherd" or "to lead." A pastor preaches, teaches, cares for, and leads the people in the church, like a shepherd cares for a flock of sheep.

"Then I will give you shepherds after my own heart, who will lead you with knowledge and understanding," (Jeremiah 3:15).

Think About It: Sometimes **pastors** are called shepherds, because they care for their people just as a shepherd cares for sheep. Jesus is known as the Good Shepherd, so it seems right that a **pastor** would also be known as a shepherd, since the **pastor** shares Jesus' love with others. What is something you appreciate about your **pastor?** Tell your **pastor**, "thank you" this week.

Patriarch (PAY-tree-ahrk)

ME: A respected or honored man in the early history of a nation or family. Abraham Isaac, Jacob, and Jacob's 12 sons are the **patriarchs** of Israel.

PT: A respected or honored man or the father of a family or tribe of people. The biblical **patriarchs** were Abraham, Isaac, Jacob, and Jacob's 12 sons.

"The LORD had said to Abram, 'Leave your country, your people and your father's household and go to the land I will show you. I will make you into a great nation and I will bless you; I will make your name great, and you will be a blessing,'" (Genesis 12:1-2).

Think About It: Abraham is a **patriarch** of our faith. We respect him as a man chosen by God. Who is someone that you look up to and respect?

Peace with God (PEES with GAHD)

EE: Knowing God has forgiven your sins and accepts you as His child. We can have **peace with God** even when bad things happen.

*"Glory to God in the highest, and on earth **peace** to men on whom his favor rests,"* *(Luke 2:14).*

Think About It: Ask someone you know to tell you about a time when they felt God's **peace** even in a difficult situation.

Peacemaker (PEES-MAYK-er)

PT: One who tries to help people who are angry or upset with each other to get along peacefully.

"Make every effort to live in **peace** *with all men and to be holy; without holiness no one will see the Lord,"* (Hebrews 12:14).

Think About It: How can you live in **peace** with others? What are some ways you can help to be a **peacemaker** with your family and friends?

Pentecost (PEN-tuh-kawst)

EE: **Pentecost** means 50. **Pentecost** Sunday is 50 days after Easter Sunday. This is when Christians celebrate the coming of the Holy Spirit and the beginning of the Church.

ME/PT: A Jewish religious festival held 50 days after Passover. Christians celebrate this as the day the Holy Spirit came and the Early Church was born.

"God, who knows the heart, showed that he accepted them by giving the Holy Spirit to them, just as he did to us. He made no distinction between us and them, for he purified their hearts by faith," (Acts 15:8-9).

Think About It: We celebrate **Pentecost** today, remembering that the Holy Spirit is God's gift to us. He is with us. He helps us to live for God and make right choices. How do you know the Holy Spirit is working in your life, helping you to make right choices?

Perish (PAIR-ish)

PT: To die. Those who die without a relationship with God are separated from Him forever.

"For the LORD watches over the way of the righteous, but the way of the wicked will **perish**,*"* (Psalm 1:6).

Think About It: How terrible to be forever separated from God. It is even difficult to imagine! What keeps you from **perishing**?

Persecution
(PER-suh-KYEW-shun)

ME: Physical abuse, ridicule, or other suffering a person experiences from others because of what he or she believes.

PT: Physical abuse, ridicule, or other suffering a person experiences from others. Christians have been and still are **persecuted** for believing in Christ and obeying Him.

*"We work hard with our own hands. When we are cursed, we bless; when we are **persecuted**, we endure it; when we are slandered, we answer kindly,"* (1 Corinthians 4:12-13a).

Think About It: Who do you know or have heard about who have been **persecuted** for believing in and choosing to follow Christ? Have you ever faced **persecution**?

Perseverance (PER-suh-VIR-uns)

PT: To do something and not stop doing it, even if it is difficult. Christians show **perseverance** when they are faithful to Jesus Christ even in tough times or in times of persecution.

*"Therefore, since we are surrounded by such a great cloud of witnesses, let us throw off everything that hinders and the sin that so easily entangles, and let us run with **perseverance** the race marked out for us,"* (Hebrews 12:1).

Think About It: Who sets your course? Who is the one that marks the race you are to run? How does knowing the one who leads you, help you to have **perseverance**?

Pharisees (FAIR-uh-SEEZ)

ME: The Jewish religious group that strictly followed the Law of Moses, and added many other rules and customs to it.

*"For whoever exalts himself will be humbled, and whoever humbles himself will be exalted. 'Woe to you, teachers of the law and **Pharisees**, you hypocrites! You shut the kingdom of heaven in men's faces. You yourselves do not enter, nor will you let those enter who are trying to,'" (Matthew 23:12-13).*

Think About It: Jesus spoke these words to the **Pharisees**. Do you ever wonder why Jesus spoke to them in this way? What do you think that Jesus was trying to tell them? What can you learn from the **Pharisees**?

Poor in spirit (POR in SPIR-it)

PT: Humble. People who are **poor in spirit** realize they can't do anything good without God's help. They depend on God instead of proudly depending on themselves.

*"Blessed are the **poor in spirit**, for theirs is the kingdom of heaven," (Matthew 5:3).*

Think About It: What is something that you know you absolutely need God's help to do?

Power (POW-ur)

EC: God has great **power**. He is more powerful than anything or anyone. He can do great things. You may also use the term "God's power."

*"His [God's] wisdom is profound, his **power** is vast. Who has resisted him and come out unscathed?" (Job 9:4).*

Think About It: How overwhelmingly awesome is God? Think of the most powerful thing or person that you can imagine. Then think about how this thing or person cannot even come close to God's great **power**. How might you describe God's **power** to someone else?

Praise (PRAYZ)

EC: To celebrate and thank God.

ME: To glorify God for who He is and all He does. We can **praise** God through our words, songs, prayer, and obedience.

*"The LORD is my strength and my song; he has become my salvation. He is my God, and I will **praise** him, my father's God, and I will exalt him," (Exodus 15:2).*

Think About It: What are some ways that you **praise** God? Choose one way to express your **praise** to God today and do it.

Pray/Prayer (PRAY/PRAYR)

EC: Talking with God.

EE: When people and God talk together and listen to one another.

ME/PT: A conversation with God that includes both talking and listening. We can **pray** anytime, anywhere, about anything

*"If my people, who are called by my name, will humble themselves and **pray** and seek my face and turn from their wicked ways, then will I hear from heaven and will forgive their sin and will heal their land,"* (2 Chronicles 7:14).

Think About It: What do you need to talk with God about today? He hears and will listen. How do you see God's answers to your **prayers**?

Prevenient grace (pree-VEEN-yunt GRAYS)

PT: God's love and mercy reaching out to all people before they know Him or want Him. **Prevenient grace** makes it possible for all people to turn to God for salvation.

*"The law was added so that the trespass might increase. But where sin increased, **grace** increased all the more, so that, just as sin reigned in death, so also **grace** might reign through righteousness to bring eternal life through Jesus Christ our Lord,"* (Romans 5:20-21).

Think About It: God loves you. Look at your reflection in a mirror. Who do you see? A person who is loved by God? God loves you. Say this to yourself at least three times today. It is because of God's love and **grace** that you can love and obey Him.

Priest (PReST)

PI: A person who represents God to the people and represents the people to God. **Priests** in the Bible offered sacrifices to God for people.

*"So Christ also did not take upon himself the glory of becoming a high **priest**. But God said to him, 'You are my Son; today I have become your Father.' And he says in another place, 'You are a **priest** forever, in the order of Melchizedek,'" (Hebrews 5:5-6).*

Think About It: The **priesthood** of the Old Testament was replaced by Jesus. The offering of sacrifices are no longer necessary. You can go directly to God through Jesus. What do you think is the best thing about being able to talk directly with God?

Promise (PRAHM-is)

EC: Keeping a **promise** is doing what we say we will do. God always does what He says. God keeps His **promises**.

EE: To give your word that you will or will not do something. In the Bible, God makes **promises**. God always does what He says He will do.

ME/PT: To give your word that you will or will not do something. God always does what He says He will do.

*"O Sovereign LORD, you are God! Your words are trustworthy, and you have **promised** these good things to your servant," (2 Samuel 7:28).*

Think About It: When God makes a **promise**, He keeps it. Just as King David trusted God, so can you. How do you show trust in God each day?

Prophecy (PRAHF-uh-see)

ME: A message from God to people. Some **prophecies** tell what will happen in the future.

PT: A message from God to people. Some **prophecies** tell what will happen in the future. However, most Bible **prophecies** tell God's thoughts about our behavior and His promises to bless those who obey Him or punish those who rebel.

*"For **prophecy** never had its origin in the will of man, but men spoke from God as they were carried along by the Holy Spirit," (2 Peter 1:21).*

Think About It: What are some messages that God has for people? How can you find these messages in the Bible?

Prophet (PRAH-fut)

EE: Someone God has chosen to receive and give special messages from Him.

ME: Someone God has chosen to receive and deliver His messages to people. A **prophet** speaks for God.

*"We have not listened to your servants the **prophets**, who spoke in your name to our kings, our princes and our fathers, and to all the people of the land," (Daniel 9:6).*

Think About It: There were several times in the Bible when God sent a **prophet** to speak to His people and they rejected God's message. How can you know when someone is sharing a message from God with you?

Pure in heart
(PYOOR in HAHRT)

PT: Being completely motivated by the desire to honor and glorify God.

*"Blessed are the **pure in heart**, for they will see God," (Matthew 5:8).*

Think About It: What is the promise that is given for those who are **pure in heart**, honoring and glorifying God? How can you honor God?

Redeem (ree-DEEM)

ME: To rescue someone from hardship or slavery and set that person free.

PT: To rescue someone from hardship or slavery and set that person free. Jesus came to **redeem** us from slavery to sin so we could love and serve God.

*"For the grace of God that brings salvation has appeared to all men. It teaches us to say "No" to ungodliness and worldly passions, and to live self-controlled, upright and godly lives in this present age, while we wait for the blessed hope—the glorious appearing of our great God and Savior, Jesus Christ, who gave himself for us to **redeem** us from all wickedness and to purify for himself a people that are his very own, eager to do what is good,"* (Titus 2:11-14).

Think About It: If you know you are **redeemed** or rescued to live for God, how will your everyday life look to others?

Redeemer (ree-DEEM-er)

PT: Someone who helps or sets free another person who cannot otherwise be redeemed. Christ is our **redeemer**.

*"I know that my **Redeemer** lives, and that in the end he will stand upon the earth,"* (Job 19:25).

Think About It: Job spoke with confidence even when facing tremendous loss and tragedy. Why? Because he knew the truth of the living God. God is with you. He saves you. You can depend upon Him. What is one thing you want to ask God for help with? You can ask!

Refuge (reh-FEWJ)

ME: A place of safety in a time of danger.

*"I love you, O Lord, my strength. The Lord is my rock, my fortress and my deliverer; my God is my rock, in whom I take **refuge**. He is my shield and the horn of my salvation, my stronghold," (Psalm 18:1-2).*

Think About It: God is our greatest **refuge**. You can be safe with Him. How is God a source of safety for you?

Regeneration (REE-jen-er-AY-shun)

PT: God's action to give spiritual life to repentant sinners. Through the Holy Spirit God changes people inwardly so they want Him in their lives, can stop sinning, and can live the Christian life.

"Now that you have purified yourselves by obeying the truth so that you have sincere love for your brothers, love one another deeply, from the heart. For you have been born again, not of perishable seed, but of imperishable, through the living and enduring word of God," (1 Peter 1:22-23).

Think About It: Have you accepted Jesus as Lord and Savior? Yes? Then you are a changed or **regenerated** person! You have been given a new life in Christ. You live to serve Him and others too. How can you serve someone in love?

Repent/Repentance
(ree-PENT/ree-PEN-tuns)

ME/PT: To turn away from sin and turn to God. To feel sorry for sin, ask for forgiveness, and decide to live for God.

*"**Repent**, then, and turn to God, so that your sins may be wiped out, that times of refreshing may come from the Lord, and that he may send the Christ, who has been appointed for you—even Jesus," (Acts 3:19-20).*

Think About It: How do you live for God each day? What is something that you have done to show that you have turned to God and away from sin?

Restitution (RES-tuh-TEW-shun)

ME/PT: The act of making things right when you have done wrong.

*"The LORD said to Moses, 'Say to the Israelites: "When a man or woman wrongs another in any way and so is unfaithful to the LORD, that person is guilty and must confess the sin he has committed. He must make full **restitution** for his wrong, add one fifth to it and give it all to the person he has wronged,"'" (Numbers 5:5-7).*

Think About It: When you hurt someone else, you do not just hurt that person. You are also doing wrong against God. That is why if you wrong someone it is very important to make things right with that person and with God.

Resurrection
(REZ-uh-REK-shun)

EE: When God made Jesus alive again after His enemies killed Him.

ME/PT: A return to life after death. Jesus was resurrected from the dead and lives today. His **resurrection** is the source of the Christian's hope for **resurrection** and eternal life.

*"Jesus said to her, 'I am the **resurrection** and the life. He who believes in me will live, even though he dies; and whoever lives and believes in me will never die. Do you believe this?'" (John 11:25-26).*

Think About It: How do you feel about Jesus' **resurrection** and your hope for eternal life? Express this feeling to God.

Revere (reh-VEER)

ME: To feel great honor and respect toward someone or something, and to show this in words or actions.

*"But for you who **revere** my name, the sun of righteousness will rise with healing in its wings. And you will go out and leap like calves released from the stall," (Malachi 4:2).*

Think About It: Does this verse make you think of great happiness? There is great joy for those who **revere** the Lord.

Reverence (REV-er-uns)

PT: An attitude of deep respect. We love, respect, and adore God.

*"But I, by your great mercy, will come into your house; in **reverence** will I bow down toward your holy temple," (Psalm 5:7).*

Think About It: The only proper attitude toward God is a deep **reverence**. What do you think this means to how we behave toward and speak to Him?

Righteous (RIE-chus)

EF: Right with God. **Righteous** people have trusted God to forgive their sins. They obey God.

ME: To be in right relationship with God, and to obey Him because of that relationship. To be Christlike and right in thoughts, words, and actions.

PT: To be in right relationship with God, and to obey Him because of that relationship. To be right or good in thoughts, words, actions. **Righteousness** also includes the desire for all people to experience what is right—justice. *See also righteousness for use of this same definition.*

*"Let the **righteous** rejoice in the LORD and take refuge in him; let all the upright in heart praise him! (Psalm 64:10).*

Think About It: There is nothing you can do to be **righteous** on your own. God makes you **righteous**. God gives you the strength to live right with Him. Thank Him for this amazing gift.

Righteousness (RIE-chus-nes)

PT: To be in right relationship with God, and to obey Him because of that relationship. To be right or good in thoughts, words, actions. **Righteousness** also includes the desire for all people to experience what is right—justice.

*"This is what the LORD says: 'Let not the wise man boast of his wisdom or the strong man boast of his strength or the rich man boast of his riches, but let him who boasts boast about this: that he understands and knows me, that I am the LORD, who exercises kindness, justice and **righteousness** on earth, for in these I delight,' declares the LORD," (Jeremiah 9:23-24).*

Think About It: How do you learn what is right, good, and just? Who is the One who helps you to live in **righteousness** each day?

Sabbath (SAB-uth)

EE: The day God set aside for rest, worship, and doing good.

ME/PT: The day God set aside for rest, worship, and doing good. For Jews, the **Sabbath** is the seventh day (Saturday). Christians celebrate the Lord's Day (Sunday) as their **Sabbath**, since this is the day Jesus rose from the dead.

*"Say to the Israelites, 'You must observe my **Sabbaths**. This will be a sign between me and you for the generations to come, so you may know that I am the LORD, who makes you holy,"* (Exodus 31:13).

Think About It: What are some special ways that you observe the **Sabbath**, or the Lord's Day? How do you set it apart as a special time?

Sacrament (SAK-ruh-munt)

PT: A symbolic act Jesus commanded Christians to do that uses physical materials to show outwardly what God has done for us or is doing in us. God is present with us in a special way when we take part in the **sacraments**. Because of this, **sacraments** are called "means of grace." The two **sacraments** Nazarenes observe are baptism and communion.

"Those who accepted his message were baptized, and about three thousand were added to their number that day. They devoted themselves to the apostles' teaching and to the fellowship, to the breaking of bread and to prayer," (Acts 2:41-42).

Think About It: Have you participated in the **sacrament** of baptism or communion? How would you describe this to someone else? What special closeness to God have you experienced because of your participation?

Sacred (SAY-krud)

ME: Someone or something that is set apart for, belongs to God, and made holy.

*"Don't you know that you yourselves are God's temple and that God's Spirit lives in you? If anyone destroys God's temple, God will destroy him; for God's temple is **sacred**, and you are that temple,"* (1 Corinthians 3:16-17).

Think About It: If being **sacred** is being set apart for God, and you are His **sacred** temple, what does that mean for your life? How can you live holy and set apart for God?

Sacrifice (SAK-ruh-FIES)

EE: A special gift that we give to God.

ME: To give up something important or to do something difficult in order to please God. A special gift given to God.

PT: To give up something important or valuable, or to do something difficult in order to please God. The word **sacrifice** also means the thing that has been offered up.

*"Therefore, I urge you, brothers, in view of God's mercy, to offer your bodies as living **sacrifices**, holy and pleasing to God—this is your spiritual act of worship. Do not conform any longer to the pattern of this world, but be transformed by the renewing of your mind. Then you will be able to test and approve what God's will is—his good, pleasing and perfect will,"* (Romans 12:1-2).

Think About It: How might you look at yourself and how you live differently when you see yourself as a living **sacrifice** or gift to God?

Salvation (sal-VAY-shun)

EE: All that God does to forgive people of their sins and to help them obey Him.

ME/PT: Everything God does to take away sins and create a right relationship between himself and a person. God sent His Son, Jesus, who died on the Cross and became our Savior. Those who ask Jesus to be their Savior receive **salvation** as a free gift.

*"Yet now I am happy, not because you were made sorry, but because your sorrow led you to repentance. For you became sorrowful as God intended and so were not harmed in any way by us. Godly sorrow brings repentance that leads to **salvation** and leaves no regret, but worldly sorrow brings death," (2 Corinthians 7:9-10).*

Think About It: When you realize how your disobedience hurts God, you become repentant or sorry. This is what leads you to want to be **saved** and to live in obedience to Him. How can your obedient actions bring happiness to God?

Sanctification (SANG-tuh-fuh-KAY-shun)

PT: The process in which God makes a person holy. It begins when a person becomes a Christian and receives the Holy Spirit. It leads to the point of entire sanctification and continues as the Christian grows in grace.

*"And that is what some of you were. But you were washed, you were **sanctified**, you were justified in the name of the Lord Jesus Christ and by the Spirit of our God," (1 Corinthians 6:11).*

Think About It: How do you see God at work, **sanctifying** you, and making you holy or more like Him each day?

Sanctify (SANG-tuh-fie)

PT: To make holy or separate from sin for God's service.

*"May God himself, the God of peace, **sanctify** you through and through. May your whole spirit, soul and body be kept blameless at the coming of our Lord Jesus Christ. The one who calls you is faithful and he will do it," (1 Thessalonians 5:23-24).*

Think About It: On your own you cannot be holy. This is something God brings about in you through His power. Ask God to help you live a holy life, completely for Him.

Sanctuary (SANG-chew-AIR-ee)

EE: A place to worship God. This is set apart and treated as special.

*"'Observe my Sabbaths and have reverence for my **sanctuary**. I am the LORD,'" (Leviticus 19:30).*

Think About It: How do you show reverence and respect for God's **sanctuary**?

Saved (SAYVD)

EE: A person who has accepted Christ as Savior and lives for Him.

*"'And everyone who calls on the name of the Lord will be **saved**,'" (Acts 2:21).*

Think About It: Do you know and accept Jesus as Lord and Savior? If not, would you like to? Talk to someone about how to pray and seek Jesus as Savior.

Savior (SAYV-yer)

EE: A **savior** sets people free from something bad. Jesus is our **Savior**. He came to earth to show us God's love. He died to set us free from our sins.

ME/PT: A **savior** rescues someone from difficulty, danger, or harm. God sent His Son, Jesus, to be our **Savior**. He died for the sins of all people. When we trust Him as our **Savior** He rescues us from sin and the spiritual harm and punishment it brings.

*"This is a trustworthy saying that deserves full acceptance (and for this we labor and strive), that we have put our hope in the living God, who is the **Savior** of all men, and especially of those who believe," (1 Timothy 4:9-10).*

Think About It: In whom do you have hope of salvation? How do you know this hope to be true?

Second coming (SEK-und KUM-ing)

ME/PT: The time when Jesus will come back to earth. Evil will be destroyed and Jesus will reign.

*"'Men of Galilee,' they said, 'why do you stand here looking into the sky? This same Jesus, who has been taken from you into heaven, will **come back** in the same way you have seen him go into heaven,'"* (Acts 1:11).

Think About It: God keeps His promises. This is why we trust that Jesus will **come again** and we will live forever in God's kingdom.

Sin (SIN)

EE: Disobeying God. We **sin** if we do something God said not to do. We also **sin** if we don't do what God said to do.

ME: Rebellion against God. A person places his or her own will above God's will and chooses to disobey God.

PT: Rebellion against God. Putting your own will above God's will and choosing to disobey Him. **Sin** can refer to a person's spiritual condition or to an action.

*"My dear children, I write this to you so that you will not sin. But if anybody does **sin**, we have one who speaks to the Father in our defense—Jesus Christ, the Righteous One. He is the atoning sacrifice for our **sins**, and not only for ours but also for the **sins** of the whole world," (1 John 2:1-2).*

Think About It: You can choose to obey God and follow His teachings. How? Ask for God's help.

Son of God (SUN of GAHD)

EE: A special name for Jesus. This name says that Jesus is God. When we know Jesus, we know God.

*"Then those who were in the boat worshiped him, saying, 'Truly you are the **Son of God**,'" (Matthew 14:33).*

Think About It: What do you know about Jesus? Who is He? What are His characteristics? When you know Jesus, the **Son of God**, you know God. Tell someone something you know to be true about Jesus.

Son of Man (SUN of MAN)

ME: A name Jesus used to describe himself. It indicates that Jesus is God's Son but He is also fully human.

*"When Jesus came to the region of Caesarea Philippi, he asked his disciples, 'Who do people say the **Son of Man** is?' They replied, 'Some say John the Baptist; others say Elijah; and still others, Jeremiah or one of the prophets.' 'But what about you?' he asked. 'Who do you say I am?' Simon Peter answered, 'You are the Christ, the Son of the living God,'"* (Matthew 16:13-16).

Think About It: Jesus is both fully God and fully human. He understands what you experience as a person. You can talk with Jesus, the **Son of Man**, about anything.

Sovereign (SAHV-run)

ME/PT: Power to rule without limits. God is **sovereign**. His power to rule is not limited in any way, except when He limits himself. He is fully in charge.

*"For you have been my hope, O **Sovereign** LORD, my confidence since my youth,"* (Psalm 71:5).

Think About It: We know that God has all power. You can depend on Him for anything.

Spiritual gifts
(SPIR-uh-chuh-wul GIFTS)

PT: Abilities given to us by God to help us do His work on earth.

*"'Now about **spiritual gifts**, brothers, I do not want you to be ignorant. There are different kinds of gifts, but the same Spirit. There are different kinds of service, but the same Lord,'" (1 Corinthians 12:1, 4-5).*

Think About It: Talk with someone about how God might use you to serve others.

Stewardship (STEW-erd-ship)

PT: The careful and responsible management of all the resources God has entrusted to our care.

*"Remember this: Whoever sows sparingly will also reap sparingly, and whoever sows generously will also reap generously. Each man should **give** what he has decided in his heart to give, not reluctantly or under compulsion, for God loves a cheerful **giver**," (2 Corinthians 9:6-7).*

Think About It: You are a good **steward** of the gifts and resources that God has given you, when you **give** back generously and with a cheerful heart to Him. What do you have to **give** to God?

Note: It is never too early to teach your child about stewardship. Talk about how everything we have belongs to God. We give back to Him out of love and obedience. These gifts can be in the form of abilities, talents, and skills; things; or money.

Submission (sub-MI-shun)

ME: Choosing to do what another person wants rather than what we want. Christians submit to God and do what He wants them to do.

*"**Submit** yourselves, then, to God. Resist the devil, and he will flee from you,"* (James 4:7).

Think About It: In what way do you **submit** to God? What is something you do because you know it pleases God?

Synagogue (SIN-uh-gahg)

PT: This is a place where the Jewish people gather to worship God. A synagogue is established when there are 10 or more males in a community. Synagogues came about in the Old Testament during the time of the exile when the Jewish people could not worship in the Temple. There is no Temple today. Jewish people still worship in communities in synagogues.

*"He taught in their **synagogues**, and everyone praised him. He went to Nazareth, where he had been brought up, and on the Sabbath day he went into the **synagogue**, as was his custom. And he stood up to read," (Luke 4:15-16).*

Think About It: Jesus taught and worshiped in the **synagogues** when He was on earth. Have you ever wondered what Jesus' teaching would have been like?

Temple (TEM-pul)

PT: A building for the worship of a god or gods. The Jerusalem Temple was a place where Jews worshiped God. Today God no longer has a Temple in Jerusalem as His dwelling place. He lives in people who have been born again through Christ.

*"What agreement is there between the **temple** of God and idols? For we are the **temple** of the living God. As God has said: 'I will live with them and walk among them, and I will be their God, and they will be my people,'" (2 Corinthians 6:16).*

Think About It: When you are a believer and follower of Jesus Christ, God lives in you. How should you see yourself? How should you treat God's **temple**?

Tempt (TEMPT)

PT: (verb) To test.

*"No temptation has seized you except what is common to man. And God is faithful; he will not let you be **tempted** beyond what you can bear. But when you are **tempted**, he will also provide a way out so that you can stand up under it," (1 Corinthians 10:13).*

Think About It: God is with you. He helps you even when you are **tempted** or tested. What is something that you have been **tempted** with?

Temptation (temp-TAY-shun)

EE: Anything that leads us to want to disobey God. **Temptation** makes disobeying God seem good and right.

ME: The desire to do something you know you shouldn't do. **Temptation** is not a sin, but it can lead to sin if you give in to it.

PT: The desire to do something you know you shouldn't do. **Temptation** is a test of a person's faithfulness to God. **Temptation** makes disobeying God seem exciting, fun, good, or right. **Temptation** is not a sin, but it can lead to sin if you give in to it.

*"Watch and pray so that you will not fall into **temptation**. The spirit is willing, but the body is weak,"* (Matthew 26:41).

Think About It: Have you ever faced a **temptation** to do wrong, to disobey God, that was really strong? What did you do?

Ten Commandments (TEN kuh-MAND-munts)

EE: Ten special rules that God gave to show us how to live as His people.

*"Then the LORD said to Moses, 'Write down these words, for in accordance with these words I have made a covenant with you and with Israel.' Moses was there with the LORD forty days and forty nights without eating bread or drinking water. And he wrote on the tablets the words of the covenant—the **Ten Commandments**,"* (Exodus 34:27-28).

Think About It: Go to Exodus Chapter 20 and read the **Ten Commandments** with your family. What are the laws that God has given to us to obey?

Testify (TES-tuh-FIE)

EE: To tell about something. People who believe in Jesus tell others that He is God's Son and came to be our Savior. This is sometimes known as Christian testimony.

*"With great power the apostles continued to **testify** to the resurrection of the Lord Jesus, and much grace was upon them all,"* (Acts 4:33).

Think About It: How do your actions **testify** to your relationship with Jesus? How can you **testify** to others with the words you use and the ways you behave?

Tithe (TIETH)

PT: A tenth of resources (income) given back to God for support of the Church.

*"Speak to the Levites and say to them: 'When you receive from the Israelites the **tithe** I give you as your inheritance, you must present a tenth of that **tithe** as the LORD's offering,'"* (Numbers 18:26).

Think About It: Everything you have comes from God. It does not belong to you. So when you give the **tithe** to Him, you are simply returning what is already His.

Transgress (tranz-GRES)

PT: To sin by disobeying God's teachings.

*"When we were overwhelmed by sins, you forgave our **transgressions**,"* (Psalm 65:3).

Think About It: If you sin, disobey God, you can go to Him and confess your **transgressions**, telling Him that you **transgressed**. He will forgive you. You can choose to obey Him.

Trinity (TRIN-uh-tee)

PT: This important Christian doctrine teaches that God is the one true God who reveals himself as three persons: God the Father, Jesus Christ the Son, and the Holy Spirit.

"The Word became flesh and made his dwelling among us. We have seen his glory, the glory of the One and Only, who came from the Father, full of grace and truth," *(John 1:14).*

"But when the kindness and love of God our Savior appeared, he saved us, not because of righteous things we had done, but because of his mercy. He saved us through the washing of rebirth and renewal by the Holy Spirit, whom he poured out on us generously through Jesus Christ our Savior," *(Titus 3:4-6).*

Think About It: Learn and say the Apostles' Creed as a family. This affirms our belief in the **Trinity**.

The Apostles' Creed

We believe in God, the Father Almighty,
the Maker of heaven and earth;

And in Jesus Christ, His only Son, our Lord:
who was conceived by the Holy Spirit,
born of the virgin Mary,
suffered under Pontius Pilate,
was crucified, dead, and buried;
He descended into hades.

The third day He arose again from the dead;

He ascended into heaven,
and sits at the right hand of God the Father Almighty;

from there He shall come to judge the living and the dead.

We believe in the Holy Spirit,
the holy Church universal,
the communion of saints,
the forgiveness of sins,
the resurrection of the body,

and the life everlasting. Amen.

Trust (TRUST)

EC: A belief that God will do what is good, fair, and helpful for us. God does what He says He will do.

EE: To believe that God is good and always keeps His promises. People who **trust** God depend on Him and obey Him.

ME: To believe that God is good and always keeps His promises. People who **trust** God depend on Him and obey Him. **Trust** is another word for faith.

PT: To put confidence in someone or something and to act upon that confidence. We **trust** God when we believe He is good and keeps His promises, then depend on and obey Him. **Trust** is another word for faith.

*"But I am like an olive tree flourishing in the house of God; I **trust** in God's unfailing love for ever and ever," (Psalm 52:8).*

Think About It: God is dependable. What does that mean to you?

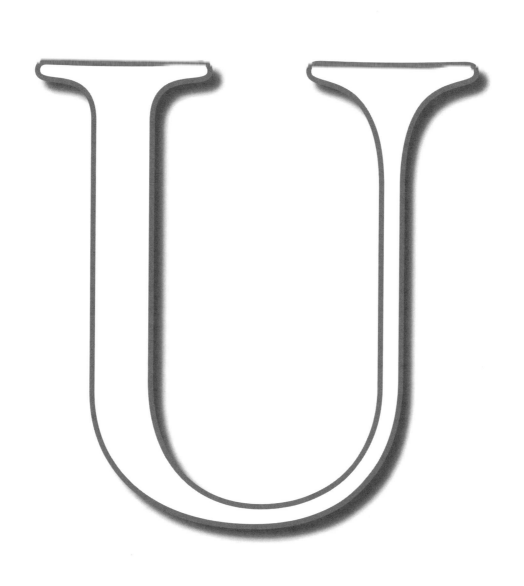

Unconditional love
(un-cun-DI-shu-nul LUV)

PT: Love that has no limitations or conditions and does not have to be earned. The person who loves unconditionally chooses to love, no matter what the other person is like or has done.

*"**Love** is patient, **love** is kind. It does not envy, it does not boast, it is not proud. It is not rude, it is not self-seeking, it is not easily angered, it keeps no record of wrongs. **Love** does not delight in evil but rejoices with the truth," (1 Corinthians 13:4-6).*

Think About It: God **loves** you and you can show His **love** to others. Read more about this **love** in 1 Corinthians, chapter 13. Then go and **love** in your words and actions.

Unity (YEW-nuh-tee)

PT: Many different parts made one. The Church experiences **unity** in Jesus Christ. The Church is made up of many different members working together to love, serve, and honor God.

*"My prayer is not for them alone. I pray also for those who will believe in me through their message, that all of them may be one, Father, just as you are in me and I am in you. May they also be in us so that the world may believe that you have sent me. I have given them the glory that you gave me, that they may be one as we are one: I in them and you in me. May they be brought to complete **unity** to let the world know that you sent me and have loved them even as you have loved me,"* *(John 17:20-23).*

Think About It: How does it make you feel to know that Jesus prayed for you? He prayed that you would be **unified** or in agreement with other believers. How does this mean we are to interact with other Christians?

Unrighteous (un-RIE-chus)

PT: To be separated from God by sin, and to live disobediently as a result. To be sinful in thoughts, desires, words, or actions.

*"For Christ died for sins once for all, the righteous for the **unrighteous**, to bring you to God. He was put to death in the body but made alive by the Spirit,"* (1 Peter 3:18).

Think About It: The only way to be made righteous is through Christ. Have you experienced the righteousness that obeying God provides?

144

Wisdom (WIZ-dum)

EE: Using what we know to make right choices. **Wisdom** comes from God

ME: The ability to use information and experiences to make right choices in daily life. **Wisdom** is a gift from God.

*"If any of you lacks **wisdom**, he should ask God, who gives generously to all without finding fault, and it will be given to him,"* (James 1:5).

Think About It: Do you have a choice to make? Ask God for the **wisdom** to make the right choice. No decision is too small or big for God's help.

Witness (WIT-nus)

ME: Someone who tells others what he or she has seen or experienced. A Christian **witness** tells others what God has done and what He means to him or her.

PT: (verb) To tell others what you have seen or experienced. To share the gospel (good news about Jesus) with someone. (noun) A Christian **witness** is a person who tells others about Jesus and salvation.

*"He came as a **witness** to testify concerning that light, so that through him all men might believe. He himself was not the light; he came only as a **witness** to the light. The true light that gives light to every man was coming into the world,"* (John 1:7-9).

Think About It: In the New Testament, John the Baptist came before to **witness** to the coming of Jesus. You are now His **witness** in the world. You are a follower and your actions and words tell others what to believe about Jesus.

Witness of the Spirit
(WIT-nus of the SPIR-it)

PT: Assurance given to Christians by the Holy Spirit that God has forgiven their sins and they are His children.

*"For you did not receive a spirit that makes you a slave again to fear, but you received the Spirit of sonship. And by him we cry, 'Abba, Father.' The **Spirit himself testifies** with our spirit that we are God's children," (Romans 8:15-16).*

Think About It: How do you experience your family's love? How do you know you belong? Who tells you this? You become a child of God when you are saved. The Holy Spirit helps you to know that you belong to Him!

Worldly passion
(WERLD-lee PA-shun)

PT: Passion is an emotion or feeling, or a strong desire. **Worldly passion** is an emotion or feeling or strong desire for whatever does not honor God.

"But mark this: There will be terrible times in the last days. People will be lovers of themselves, lovers of money, boastful, proud, abusive, disobedient to their parents, ungrateful, unholy, without love, unforgiving, slanderous, without self-control, brutal, not lovers of the good, treacherous, rash, conceited, lovers of pleasure rather than lovers of God—having a form of godliness but denying its power. Have nothing to do with them," (2 Timothy 3:1-5).

Think About It: You can make a promise to God. Promise Him that you will choose to live for Him in obedience each day. This is not something you can do on your own, but do not worry! God will help you, you just need to ask Him.

Worship (WER-shup)

PK: To praise and thank God.

FE: Telling and showing God that we love Him more than anyone or anything else.

ME: To praise God and show Him honor, reverence, or adoration. To profess that God is the ruler of our lives.

PT: To praise, show honor, reverence, or adoration. Christians are to **worship** only God and offer their whole life to Him.

*"Come, let us bow down in **worship**, let us kneel before the LORD our Maker; for he is our God and we are the people of his pasture, the flock under his care," (Psalm 95:6-7).*

Think About It: Do you love God? Do you love Him more than anyone or anything else? Then praise Him! Praise Him in the way you know best: song, art, movement. . . there are many ways that you can **worship** God.

Abomination (uh-BAHM-uh-NAY-shun)	Acceptance (ik SEP-tuns)	Accountable (uh-KOUN-tuh-bul)	Adoption (uh-DAHP-shun)
Advent (AD-vent)	Advocate (AD-vuh-kut)	Agape (ah-GAH-pay)	Altar (AWL-ter)
Anoint (uh-NOYNT)	Antichrist (AN-ti-KRIEST)	Apostle (uh-PAHS-ul)	Armor of God (AHR-mer of GAHD)
Ascension (uh-SEN-shun)	Assurance (uh-SHOOR-uns)	Atonement (uh-TOHN-munt)	Atoning sacrifice (uh-TOHN-ing SAK-ruh-fies)

Baptism (BAP-tiz-um)	**Believers** (buh-LEE-vers)	**Bible** (BIE-bul)	**Blessed** (BLESD)
Blessing (BLES-ing)	**Body of Christ** (BAH-dee of KRIEST)	**Born Again** (BOHRN uh-GEN)	**Canon** (KAN–un)
Choice(s) (CHOYS)	**Christ** (KRIEST)	**Christ/Messiah** (KRIEST/muh-SIE-uh)	**Christian** (KRIS-chun)
Christmas (KRIS-mus)	**Church** (CHERCH)	**Comforter** (KUM-fer-ter)	**Commandment** (kuh-MAND-munt)

Commit/ Commitment (kuh-MIT/ kuh-MIT-munt)	**Communion** (kuh-MYEWN-yun)	**Community** (kuh-MYEW-nuh-tee)	**Compassion** (kum-PA-shun)
Condemn (kun-DEM)	**Confess** (kun-FES)	**Consecrate** (KAHN-see-KRAYT)	**Convict** (kun-VIKT)
Conviction (kun-VIK-shun)	**Covenant** (KUV-uh-nunt)	**Covet** (KUV-it)	**Create** (kree-AYT)
Creator (kree-AY-ter)	**Creed** (KREED)	**Cross** (KRAHS)	**Crucifixion** (KREW-suh-FIK-shun)

Deity (DEE-uh-tee)	Disciple(s) (duh-SIE-pulz)	Divine (duh-VIEN)	Easter (EE-ster)
Entire Sanctification (EN-tier SANG-tuh-fuh-KAY-shun)	Eternal life (ee-TER-nul LIEF)	Eternity (ee-TER-nuh-tee)	Eucharist (YEW-kuh-rust)
Evangelism (ee-VAN-juh-liz-um)	Evil (EE-vuhl)	Exodus (EK-suh-dus)	Faith (FAYTH)
Faithful (FAYTH-ful)	Fall (FAWL)	Family of God (FAM-uh-lee of GAHD)	Fast (FAST)

Fear (FEER)	**Fellowship** (FEL-oh-ship)	**Follower of Jesus** (FAH-luh-wer of JEE-zus)	**Fool** (FEWL)
Forgive (fohr-GIV)	**Forgiveness** (fohr-GIV-nus)	**Free will** (FREE WIL)	**Friend** (FREND)
Fruit of the Spirit (FREWT of the SPIR-it)	**Gentile** (JEN-tiel)	**Glorify** (GLOH-ruh-fie)	**God** (GAHD)
Godliness (GAHD-lee-nus)	**God's care** (GAHD's KAIR)	**God's help** (GAHD's HELP)	**God's power** (GAHD's POW-er)

God's will (GAHD's WIL)	God's work (GAHD's WERK)	Golden Rule (GOHL-dun REWL)	Good Friday (GOOD FRI-day)
Good News (GOOD NEWZ)	Gospel (GAHS-pul)	Grace (GRAYS)	Gracious (GRAY-shus)
Growth in grace (GROHTH in GRAYS)	Hallowed (HAL-oh-ed)	Heart (HAHRT)	Heaven (HEV-un)
High Priest (HIE PREEST)	Holiness (HOH-lee-nus)	Holy (HOH-lee)	Holy Spirit (HOH-lee SPIR-ut)

Honor (ON-er)	Hope (HOHP)	Hypocrisy (hi-PAHK-ruh-see)	Idol (IE-dul)
Image of God (IM-ij of GAHD)	Immanuel (i-MAN-yuh-wul)	Incarnation (IN-kahr-NAY-shun)	Inspiration (IN-spuh-RAY-shun)
Intercede (IN-ter-SEED)	Jealousy (JEL-uh-see)	Jesus (JEE-zus)	Joy (JOY)
Judge (JUJ)	Judgment (JUJ-munt)	Justification (JUS-tuh-fuh-KAY-shun)	Kingdom of God (KING-dum of GAHD)

Law (LAW)	Lord's Prayer (LOHRDZ PRAYR)	Lord's Supper (LOHRDZ SUP-er)	Love (LUV)
Mediator (MEE-dee-AY-ter)	Meek (MEEK)	Mercy (MER-see)	Messiah (muh-SIE-uh)
Miracle (MIR-uh-kul)	Missionary (MISH-uh-NAIR-ee)	Missions (MISH-uns)	Mourn (MORN)
Obedience (oh-BEE-dee-uns)	Obey (oh-BAY)	Offering (AWF-er-ing)	Original sin (uh-RIJ-uh-nul SIN)

Outreach (OUT-REECH)	**Pagan** (PAY-gun)	**Palm Sunday** (PAHM SUN-dee)	**Parable(s)** (PAIR-uh-buls)
Pardon (PAHR-dun)	**Passover** (PAS-OH-ver)	**Pastor** (PAS-ter)	**Patriarch** (PAY-tree-ahrk)
Peace with God (PEES with GAHD)	**Peacemaker** (PEES-MAYK-er)	**Pentecost** (PEN-tuh-kawst)	**Perish** (PAIR-ish)
Persecution (PER-suh-KYEW-shun)	**Perseverance** (PER-suh-VIR-uns)	**Pharisees** (FAIR-uh-SEEZ)	**Poor in spirit** (POR in SPIR-it)

Power (POW-ur)	Praise (PRAYZ)	Pray/Prayer (PRAY/PRAYR)	Prevenient grace (pree-VEEN-yunt GRAYS)
Priest (PREEST)	Promise (PRAHM-is)	Prophecy (PRAHF-uh-see)	Prophet (PRAH-fut)
Pure in heart (PYOOR in HAHRT)	Redeem (ree-DEEM)	Redeemer (ree-DEEM-er)	Refuge (reh-FEWJ)
Regeneration (REE-jen-er-AY-shun)	Repent/ Repentance (ree-PENT/ ree-PEN-tuns)	Restitution (RES-tuh-TEW-shun)	Resurrection (REZ-uh-REK-shun)

Revere (reh-VEER)	Reverence (REV-er-uns)	Righteous (RIE-chus)	Righteousness (RIE-chus-nes)
Sabbath (SAB-uth)	Sacrament (SAK-ruh-munt)	Sacred (SAY-krud)	Sacrifice (SAK-ruh-FIES)
Salvation (sal-VAY-shun)	Sanctification (SANG-tuh-fuh-KAY-shun)	Sanctify (SANG-tuh-fie)	Sanctuary (SANG-chew-AIR-ee)
Saved (SAYVD)	Savior (SAYV-yer)	Second coming (SEK-und KUM-ing)	Sin (SIN)

Son of God (SUN of GAHD)	Son of Man (SUN of MAN)	Sovereign (SAHV-run)	Spiritual gifts (SPIR-uh-chuh-wul GIFTS)
Stewardship (STEW-erd-ship)	Submission (sub-MI-shun)	Synagogue (SIN-uh-gahg)	Temple (TEM-pul)
Tempt (TEMPT)	Temptation (temp-TAY-shun)	Ten Commandments (TEN kuh-MAND-munts)	Testify (TES-tuh-FIE)
Tithe (TIETH)	Transgress (tranz-GRES)	Trinity (TRIN-uh-tee)	Trust (TRUST)

Unconditional love (un-cun-DI-shu-nul LUV)	Unity (YEW-nuh-tee)	Unrighteous (un-RIE-chus)	Wisdom (WIZ-dum)
Witness (WIT-nus)	Witness of the Spirit (WIT-nus of the SPIR-it)	Worldly passion (WERLD-lee PA-shun)	Worship (WER-shup)